SPIRITUAL DISCERNMENT WORKSHOP

COLETTE TOACH

AMI BOOKSHOP
www.ami-bookshop.com

Spiritual Discernment Workshop

ISBN-10: 1-62664-144-7
ISBN-13: 978-1-62664-144-0

Copyright © 2016 by Apostolic Movement International, LLC
All rights reserved
5663 Balboa Ave #416,
San Diego,
California 92111,
United States of America

1st Printing 2016

Published by **Apostolic Movement International, LLC**
E-mail Address: admin@ami-bookshop.com
Web Address: www.ami-bookshop.com

All rights reserved under International Copyright Law.
Contents may not be reproduced in whole or in part in any form without the express written consent of the publisher.

Unless specified, all Scripture references taken from the New King James Version®. Copyright © 1982 by Thomas Nelson. Used by permission. All rights reserved.

Foreword

History was not one of my favorite subjects in school. To be really honest, all those dates and names just gave me a headache.

It was only until we started traveling, did I come to love the lessons that could be learned by those who had lived before me. Going to old castles and seeing how they lived and what they had to do to live, gave me a renewed appreciation of how we benefit from their trials and successes.

Just look at the dark ages. It was a time in history that not many like to look at, but it was a lack of knowledge that kept those people in bondage and they were unable to break free.

It was the industrial revolution and the development of the printing press that forced change. This very event allowed bibles to be read by everyone and not just clergymen. This allowed common people to know that there was more they could expect from the life that they were living.

The Church right now is facing a similar situation when it comes to the spiritual and demonic realm. There is so much that is being said, and so many people are doing outrageous things in the name of the Lord. Yet, without wisdom, understanding, and discernment from the Holy Spirit, there is no way to really tell what is really of the Lord Jesus, and what is the counterfeit of the enemy.

That is why we put this book together. We want to bring to you the best opportunity to discern for yourself the right from the wrong, and to bring this change to the Church. We want you to know when the Lord Jesus is moving, and when to stand against the enemy.

To do this, we have taken excerpts from some of our books and condensed them into this powerful tool and weapon. With this book, I know you will find the righteous anger of the Lord Jesus rising up in you when you see the heresy that is taking place in the Church. Yet, it will also give you the heart of your loving Savior for the hurt and the broken.

With this balance, you will become the new type of warrior that will change the face of the Church, and lead it into the new and blessed season the Lord Jesus wants her to be in.

So as you read these pages, let it challenge you. Let this book anoint you for the bigger work at hand, but best of all, let it make you the light in the darkness that will draw those seeking the Lord to you. Then, you can show them the real Lord Jesus and the love from Him that they are so desperately seeking.

This is your recipe for blessing and success wherever you go!

Much love and blessing,

Craig Toach

Co-Founder
Apostolic Movement International

Contents

Foreword 3

Chapter 01 – How to Hear God's Voice for Yourself 10
    Using the Urim and Thummim 12
    Knowing With the Spirit 13
    Flowing in Visions 14
    Journaling 16
    Scriptures to Memorize 18
    Key Principles 18
    Practical Application 18
    Extra Notes: 21

Chapter 02 – The Gift of Discerning of Spirits 24
    How the Prophet ROCKS the Gift of Discerning of Spirits 26
    Scriptures to Memorize 31
    Key Principles 31
    Practical Application 32
    Extra Notes: 35

Chapter 03 – Dealing with Demons and Deception 38
    Play it Safe 39
    The Spirit of Divination 39
    How Deception Comes 43
    Avoiding Deception 47
    Signs of Deception 49
    Scriptures to Memorize 53
    Key Principles 53
    Practical Application: 53
    Extra Notes 57

Chapter 04 – Dealing with Demonic Manifestations 60
    Two Camps 61

    Demon Manifestations 62

    Setting Someone Free 65

    Some Signs of Demonic Bondage 67

    Scriptures to Memorize 70

    Key Principles 70

    Practical Application: 70

    Extra Notes 72

Chapter 05 – Nightmares, Deception and Demonic Dreams 74

    Identifying Deception 74

    3 Categories of Deceptive Dreams 74

    Scriptures to Memorize 80

    Key Principles 80

    Practical Application: 80

    Extra Notes 82

Chapter 06 – Satanic Attack in Dreams 84

    Practicalities 86

    Scripture to Memorize 94

    Key Principles 94

    Practical Application: 94

    Extra Notes 96

Chapter 07 – Logic, Deception, and Spirit of Divination Checklist 98

    Extra Notes 102

Chapter 08 – The Prophetic Super Spy 104

    Demonic Bondage 105

    Demonic Oppression vs. Demonic Possession 105

    Demonic Oppression 105

    Demonic Possession 107

    Scriptures to Memorize 116

    Key Principles 116

    Practical Application: 117

Extra Notes 118

Chapter 09 – Satan's Kingdom – Principalities and Powers 120

- Principalities 121
- Powers 123
- Scriptures to Memorize 126
- Key Principles 126
- Practical Application: 126
- Extra Notes 128

Chapter 10 – Satan's Kingdom – Rulers and Princes 130

- Rulers 130
- Wickedness in High Places - Princes 137
- Principalities, Powers, Rulers, Princes 143
- Scriptures to Memorize 145
- Key Principles 145
- Practical Application: 146
- Extra Notes 148

Chapter 11 – The Difference Between Curses and Spiritual Warfare 150

- The Arrows – A Picture of Spiritual Warfare 150
- The Crack in the Wall - Your Personal Sin 150
- No Need to Fear 152
- Scriptures to Memorize 154
- Key Principles 154
- Practical Application: 154
- Extra Notes 156

Chapter 12 – Step–by–Step Solutions 158

- Dealing With Generational Curses 158
- Dealing With Leaven 160
- Dealing with Personal Sin 162
- Practical Project 163
- Quick Note on Doctrine 165

- Scriptures to Memorize 166
- Key Principles 166
- Extra Notes 167

Bonus Chapter – Dealing With a Backlash 170
- How does it happen? 171
- How do you prevent it? 172
- Scriptures to Memorize 173
- Key Principles 173

About the Author 174

Excerpts Taken From the Following Books 175
- Prophetic Warrior 175
- Prophetic Counter Insurgence 175
- The Minister's Handbook 176
- Prophetic Essentials 176
- The Way of Dreams and Visions 177
- Strategies of War 177
- The Way of Dreams and Visions Student Manual 178
- Practical Prophetic Ministry Student Manual 178

Contact Information United States 179

Contact Information South Africa 180

CHAPTER 01

HOW TO HEAR GOD'S VOICE FOR YOURSELF

Chapter 01 – How to Hear God's Voice for Yourself

Chapter Reference: *The Minister's Handbook*, Chapter 2

Do you know what I hated the most about dating? It was that you had to try and snatch your moments of time together. Do you remember what it was to be in love for the first time? You wanted to spend every possible minute with that person.

Unfortunately, though all you got were these snatches. For many of us, we were still living with our parents and of course there were curfews and annoying things like school or work that got in the way. So, what you did was try to snatch as much time as you could with the person you loved.

Craig and I were no different when we were dating. We would go late into the night sharing our hearts, pushing the boundaries until we had spent every last minute we could together. He would drop me off at home and then we would stand outside the front door talking until we really had to go our separate ways.

The most incredible thing about being married was that you could spend the whole night and day together. No more limitations!

This is the same progress your relationship takes as you get to know the Lord. As you first start to hear the voice of the Lord for yourself, it is like grabbing little snatches of His time. You learn to hear His voice through impressions in your spirit or through the Word. However, grabbing those snatches and really living with Him are two separate things all together.

As you come to pouring out to others and ministering to them, your relationship with the Lord is going to go up a notch. So in this chapter I want to teach you how to do just that. I want to take you past grabbing just snatches of time with the Lord and to walking in a full, love relationship with Him.

Many folks think that hearing the voice of the Lord is a special event whereby you have to wait until He graces you with a Word. You could not be further from the truth! The Lord is talking to you all the time, and just because you cannot hear Him, does not mean that He is silent.

MOVING BEYOND THE COURTING STAGE

Now as you come to minister to others, you will need to hear the Lord more than ever. Those snatches you have had with Him before just do not cut it. Now you might be new in your walk with the Lord or you might have walked with Him for years. Either way, I am calling you into a deeper revelation of the Lord.

As the Lord uses you more in ministry, you need to be able to hear His voice more. You need to be sure of the revelation that you receive. This can only come with a more intimate relationship with the Lord. It is time to move beyond the courting stage and onto a closer intimacy with the Lord.

You cannot try to tell God's people how to hear His voice for themselves, if you cannot hear it for yourself first!

That would be a bit like a mechanic sending his own car to another mechanic to be fixed. How can you introduce the Church to a Groom that you do not know for yourself?

Not only should you be able to hear His voice, but you should come to a place of rest knowing that He will always be there to speak to you when you minister. You should never feel that ministry is a "hit and miss" event where God could speak or God could be silent.

EXPECTING TO HEAR HIS VOICE

When you know the Lord intimately, you can rest assured that He will be there every time to use you. His anointing will always show up. His revelation and wisdom will always flow out.

That would be like me lying in bed at night wondering, "Is my husband going to speak to me tonight? I wonder if he will notice me lying here." Of course I can expect to hear my husband's voice. We have a covenant relationship and I expect to communicate openly with him.

Should it be any different with the Lord? You should come to the place in your spiritual walk, where you no longer wonder, "Is the Lord going to speak to me or not? Oh, I hope He notices me." Rather you should be at a place of rest knowing that He is speaking all of the time and expecting to hear Him when you need Him most.

If a husband in the natural can fulfill this simple expectation - how much more our Heavenly Bridegroom?

So let me break it down for you again and give you some simple pointers in taking your relationship with the Lord Jesus up a notch.

USING THE URIM AND THUMMIM

There were two stones in the breastplate of the high priest. So if someone wanted to hear a clear "YES" or "NO" from the Lord, they would go to the priest. The priest would then use the "Urim and Thummim" to get their answer.

This is the same Urim and Thummim used in the day of Ezra to determine if a priest was given the "yes or no" to confirm his genealogy.

> ***Ezra 2:63*** *And the governor said to them that they should not eat of the most holy things till a priest could consult with the Urim and Thummim.*

So you could go to the priest and say, "Lord, should I marry this woman?" And the Lord would answer yes or no.

Wouldn't it be handy to have a Urim and Thummim in today's day and age? Well, I have some good news for you – you do! It is called the indwelling of the Holy Spirit and He has been giving you signals for some time now.

Think over the last week or so and the different situations you faced. Were you in a situation where you just felt a hunch? A feeling that said, "DO NOT do this". Or perhaps you had a feeling in your spirit that said, "Yes! Go for it!" The "gut feel" that comes from deep down in your spirit is the same as the Urim and Thummim of the priesthood.

If you would only listen to that prompting, you would find things going a lot easier for you. You see, the Lord is speaking to you all of the time and giving you direction, you have just not been aware of it. Now it does not matter what your ministry calling is, every believer has the ability to hear God in this way.

Simply learn to listen to your spirit and not to ignore those inner promptings. When you feel a check in your spirit, it is time to stop and not push through. However, when you feel that go ahead, you can walk forward with complete confidence.

Learning to listen to your spirit can transform your day. We do not always have the opportunity to run away for a quiet time with the Lord to hear Him more clearly. In the middle of ministry or when a situation comes up, this is the time for you to listen to the promptings coming from deep within your spirit.

The more you take that moment to listen, the easier it will be to follow the leading of the Holy Spirit. It is easy to shut off and hear the Lord when you are alone, but not so easy when someone knocks at your door and needs ministry right now. This is the time to listen to what the Lord is saying through your spirit.

When the Lord is giving you a "thummim" you might have a feeling of dread or uncertainty. A thought perhaps came to you that said, "I need to take things easy here and wait for a bit." Or perhaps you felt, "I wonder if I should tell this person about..."

Think back on times when you felt that prompting and you did not obey it. Afterwards you could have kicked yourself! Well, do not make that same mistake again. Make the effort to pay attention to what is coming from your spirit instead of hopping on a track and just going with it.

THE FIRST IMPRESSION IS RIGHT!

When someone comes for ministry, you need to be sensitive to what your spirit is saying. When someone asks a question, pay attention to the first impression that you feel in your spirit. Often you push that first impression aside and try to make sense of their problem with your mind.

You ignore the promptings in your spirit and go straight to figuring out the problem with your mind. Armed with tons of great principles, you try to analyze the person and the situation instead of listening to what God is saying first.

However, in my experience that first impression was the right one! The moment you heard their question, what is the first thing you felt? Did you feel positive or negative in the spirit?

So before you even minister or try to get revelation for someone, listen to your spirit! The Urim and Thummim is like a step in the door.

KNOWING WITH THE SPIRIT

When Craig and I were dating I could never tell when he was upset with me. He was always just an amiable nice-guy and had a smile on his face. He did not like to tell me when something bothered him.

After a little while of marriage though, I knew him well enough to just glance in his direction and know, "uh oh... I put my foot in it again! I said something I should not have!"

Learning to develop this way of hearing the Lord matures as your relationship progresses with Him. You go from trying to guess what God is saying to you, to sensing clearly in your spirit if something is of Him or not.

You do not always need to get a clear word of direction from the Lord with a full map and compass. More often than not, you get promptings that are like little lights along a garden path, lighting up one after the other. If you follow them, you will reach your destination.

You do not always need a full prophetic word and revelation to get your feet moving. If my husband always had to tell me, word by word, every single thought he had, our marriage would be in a sad state of affairs. I should know him well enough to follow his lead without him always having to give me full directions.

Not only should I trust him, but I should also know him well enough to know what is on his mind. Well it is the same with the Lord. You need to develop your relationship with him to the point where you can sense a step at a time where He is leading you. Then, you will know with the spirit and so walk alongside the Lord as He leads.

Now when you hear that prompting from your spirit, you have a choice to make. You can decide to follow that prompting or ignore it and do your own thing.

Now I am not saying that you should base your entire spiritual life on this one principle, but it certainly starts leading you in the right direction. From here you can learn to communicate more with the Lord and get clearer revelation.

By learning to be aware of His voice all through the day, you will be in a better position to flow in some of the other ways.

FLOWING IN VISIONS

In many circles visions are regarded as such a spiritual experience that they do not realize that flowing in visions should be part of the daily life of every believer. You should be able to hear the Lord all of the time. Now I am not going to delve into how to flow in visions, because I put a lot of effort into that in my *Way of Dreams and Visions* book.

Instead, I want you to bring experiencing visions to the place where you are using them to hear the Lord for yourself. You should be using visions in your personal prayer time all of the time. If you took the time to flow in visions in your personal prayer times with the Lord, flowing out in ministry becomes an extension of what you do all of the time.

Now, not only prophets can flow in visions! Any believer and the Fivefold Ministry can. Combined with what I have already shared, you will feel comfortable ministering to someone.

If you want to get to know the Lord, it is going to mean listening to Him in the quiet. It means getting revelation for your life in your private prayer times.

ONE ON ONE TIME

When Craig and I were dating, we were always around a lot of people. Even though we had a good time with the group, we only got to know each other after everyone had gone home and we were alone long enough to talk. We did not base our relationship on the interaction we had in the group, but rather on our private times.

Well it is the same with the Lord. When you stand up to minister or you are counseling someone, you are interacting with the Lord in a group. You are ministering, but you are not developing your personal relationship with Him.

I want you to remember that point, because it is so easy to forget when you start getting really busy in ministry. You think that pouring out is the same as intimacy, but it is not true at all. True intimacy comes when you are alone. It is the times when you are in the secret place, listening to your spirit, journaling and flowing in visions that God gives to you, that you really get to know Him.

You will start to feel comfortable with the sound of the Lord's voice. Then when you are in the middle of a crisis or someone needs urgent ministry, you will be able to discern the Lord's voice above all of the noise around you.

NO DOUBT - MINISTRY IS SIMPLE

With this kind of relationship, you will not have to doubt if what you hear was His voice or not. When you are ministering and He speaks into your spirit, you will not need to panic and say, "Lord was that you? Lord, please confirm what you are saying. I am not sure!"

You will be sure, because you would have heard Him enough in your private times to know that He is speaking to you and through you right now.

If you do this, then next time you stand up to minister, you will have so much more to pour out. You will no longer teach or minister from principles alone, but from principles that you experienced in your day-to-day walk with Jesus.

This is true ministry! This is what it means to represent Christ to His Church.

When you minister to others, you are flowing out of what you already have in the Lord. This brings such a peace. You no longer have to strive so hard to get the revelations or the answer. You can minister out of confidence and rest.

JOURNALING

As you develop your relationship with the Lord you can also use journaling to converse with Him. The great thing about journaling is that you can document all direction and revelation that He gives to you. I am not going to give you full teaching on that here again, because we have taught it in so many other places.

When you know that you have to meet with someone for the purpose of ministry, then journaling will put everything into perspective for you. I use this myself all the time, especially when I need to speak or attend a seminar.

I do not take a step forward until I have journaled and written down what God wants to say. It is so easy to get carried away with the things that you see in the natural, that you can overlook what God wants to do.

If you are about to give someone marital counsel it is so easy to look at their problem from the outside and make your own assessment. If you have studied up on a lot of principles, then you need to journal even more!

You need the Lord to cut through all of your knowledge and to pull out the one gem and direction that you need to use. Learning to journal before jumping ahead of the Lord will help you learn to flow in that kind of wisdom.

I have found that the Lord has a way of exposing a problem that I never considered before. He knows the heart of the person you are going to minister to. He knows the exact thing that will reach them. So take the time to journal and to hear what He is telling you.

The great thing about this is that when you do step behind the pulpit or have the person in front of you, you feel confident, because God has spoken. This means you will also flow more in the anointing, because you are not trying so hard to minister, but rather just pouring out what God has already given to you.

COMING TO A PLACE OF REST

As you learn to develop your relationship with the Lord, you will become comfortable with His voice. You will sense the changes in the spirit. You will get impressions and visions and this will give you security.

You will no longer fear that God might not show up. You can trust in Him. Why? Because you know Him! You read of all the ministry greats and how well they could hear from God and often it can make you feel a bit inferior.

You can feel that you have not yet "arrived" to be able to be used in the same way. Child of God, this is a lie from the pit of hell! Jesus does not play favorites. Not only can you hear His voice, but you can also rest assured that His anointing is ready and waiting for you.

You do not need to earn it or struggle to find it. It is right within your spirit. All you need to do is learn to get it out. You do this through a relationship with Jesus. This is the same relationship that Peter had when he reached out to the crippled man and said, "Silver and gold I do not have - but what I have, I give you. In the name of Jesus Christ of Nazareth rise up and walk."

That spirit was inside of him and he knew Jesus well enough to know that Jesus wanted that man healed! All he did was act on what Jesus wanted.

You too can know what Jesus wants. Ministry is simply flowing out from that. All of the anointing and power that you could desire is wrapped up in knowing His voice. You never have to fear Him deserting you in a difficult moment.

You can rest assured that the next time you stand up to preach or minister, that He is right there alongside you, speaking into your spirit and giving you the power you need to reach His people.

This chapter was taken from the **Minister's Handbook** written by Colette Toach.

SCRIPTURES TO MEMORIZE

Ezra 2:63 And the governor said to them that they should not eat of the most holy things till a priest could consult with the Urim and Thummim.

KEY PRINCIPLES

- ✓ Urim is a "yes" feeling in your spirit and Thummim is a "no" feeling.
- ✓ Not only prophets flow in visions – everybody can.
- ✓ Journaling is a written conversation with the Lord.
- ✓ Journaling before jumping ahead of the Lord will help you learn to flow in wisdom.
- ✓ All of the anointing and power that you could desire is wrapped up in knowing His voice.

PRACTICAL APPLICATION

1. WHAT IS THE SPIRITUAL URIM AND THUMMIM?

After reading this chapter, the answer should be clear to you, but why not approach this as if you were trying to explain it to someone who had never heard of it before.

_____

_____

_____

_____

_____

2. **CAN YOU IDENTIFY TIMES IN YOUR LIFE WHEN YOU FELT EITHER A URIM OR THUMMIM?**

   Try looking at things that happened to you this week and how you felt about it. Were there times when you said to yourself, "I should have listened to my spirit and not gone there!"

   _____
   _____
   _____
   _____
   _____
   _____
   _____

3. **CAN YOU IDENTIFY FEELING EITHER OF THESE TODAY?**

   The Lord is speaking to us all of the time. Think about when you felt the Urim or Thummim as you went through your day today.

   _____
   _____
   _____
   _____
   _____
   _____

4. **WHEN YOU THINK BACK ON DIFFICULT SITUATIONS YOU GOT YOURSELF INTO IN THE PAST, CAN YOU IDENTIFY THAT NEGATIVE "NO" FEELING THAT YOU HAD? CAN YOU SEE HOW IT WAS YOUR THUMMIM IN ACTION?**

   It is vital that you learn to identify this! In the future it will guard you against bad choices and even give you a warning when not to step out in ministry.

   _____
   _____
   _____
   _____
   _____
   _____

5. **CAN YOU IDENTIFY A SITUATION IN THE PAST WHERE THE LORD LED YOU TO SPEAK OUT OR DO SOMETHING AND YOU FELT A "YES" AND "GO AHEAD" IN YOUR SPIRIT? CAN YOU IDENTIFY THAT YOUR URIM WAS IN MOTION?**

   This might have happened when the Lord gave you a revelation to share. Identify it and next time you feel it, step out in confidence.

   _____
   _____
   _____
   _____
   _____
   _____

6. **NOW THAT YOU KNOW THAT YOU HAVE A URIM AND THUMMIM, WHAT DO YOU PLAN ON DOING TO EXERCISE THIS GIFT THAT GOD HAS GIVEN YOU?**

_____
_____
_____
_____
_____
_____
_____

EXTRA NOTES:

_____
_____
_____
_____
_____
_____
_____

CHAPTER 02

THE GIFT OF DISCERNING OF SPIRITS

Chapter 02 – The Gift of Discerning of Spirits

Chapter Reference: *Prophetic Essentials*, Chapter 11 and *Practical Prophetic Ministry Student Manual*, Lesson 7

> *Acts 8:23 For I see that you are poisoned by bitterness and bound by iniquity.*

If I had to say that I had a favorite spiritual gift, this would be the one. It is my earnest desire that every believer can function in this gift. What is this gift? It is an unheard of gift that nobody ever seems to preach about…

> **KEY PRINCIPLE**
>
> It's the ability to discern the spiritual realm. The ability to discern or see the presence of angels and demons. It is also the ability to sense the condition of another human's spirit (as Peter describes for us in Acts 8:23).

It is a powerful gift. This is the gift that enables you to see angels or demons in the spirit. Not only that, this is also the gift that enables you to sense oppression and the condition of a person's human spirit.

Often somebody will write to me and I will say, "You are under oppression."

They will reply, "Well, how do you know?"

"I sensed it!"

I can sense when somebody stands up and their word is not from God. It might even sound nice and good. To take a scriptural example; how could Jeremiah tell that something was wrong when the prophets stood up to say that everything was going to be great?

He said, "Judah is going to be destroyed and your king won't be brought back. The Lord is finishing you. (Jeremiah 28)

Their word sounded so good though. Who does not want to hear such an encouraging word from God? The Lord told Jeremiah though that the others were talking rubbish and that what he had received was indeed of the Lord.

In the New Testament, we have the gift of discerning of spirits, which makes things a lot easier. This is a gift you do not see in the Old Testament and it is no wonder that the Israelites always went astray.

They only had the law to go by. They did not have this gift to help them sense spiritually when something was amiss. Instead they had to weigh everything by the Scriptures alone. We are blessed to have both in the New Testament!

So to flow in the gift of discerning of spirits, it means that when somebody gives a prophetic word or says something, we can discern the spirit on it.

It's such a powerful gift. Just imagine if every believer could discern the spirit. When some person stands up to give a false word, they could feel the oppression and would know that it is not of God. On the other hand, they could also discern when something is of God and sense the anointing on it.

DISCERNING THE ANOINTING

A lot of the time, people just have a "good feeling" and think that this is the anointing. It is not so. You need the gift of discerning of spirits to sense the anointing. You as a prophet shouldn't live without this gift because it's so powerful.

For me, I feel it in different ways. When I sense the anointing, I feel it as a warm glow and a deep peace inside. When I feel the Holy Spirit working, I feel it like butterflies in my belly. You know that churning in the pit of your stomach and the warm glow on the outside? Everyone will experience it differently.

DISCERNING OPPRESSION

When I sense oppression though it is quite different. I feel like my hair is crawling. I don't know how other people experience this. My husband, Craig also feels oppression in his hands. He says that it feels like electricity in his fingers.

He can pick up an object and physically feel the oppression on it. That is the gift of discerning of spirits at work.

Because I work more with people, I experience oppression or the anointing on a person's words very strongly. If you write me an email, I can sense immediately what is going on in your spirit.

It's the gift of discerning of spirits. Like I said, the most obvious for me is to feel it like my hair is crawling. You know that feeling like goose-bumps on your head?

That's what I feel. Now, when a demon is present, I feel this cold sensation all over. It's a horrible feeling, but then I know what's going on. I feel a heaviness or extreme weariness and I know it's demonic. That is the gift of discerning of spirits at work.

DISCERNING THE CONDITION OF ANOTHER HUMAN SPIRIT

You see, it's not just about seeing angels and demons in the spirit. It is certainly an important part to be able to sense angels and demons, but to discern another believer's spirit is incredible because it enables you to operate with power. Your ministry can go to a whole new level thanks to this gift.

I have a nasty habit of disconcerting my team with this. They pretend everything is fine, but one of them may be really going through a bit of a tough time. They put on a happy face and walk in my office and I will say, "What's wrong?"

"Nothing… why?"

"Well, I can just feel oppression. There is something up in your spirit. What's going on?"

It's true because they know they are going through some things. I sense it in their spirit. This is a very strong gift in our ministry.

When people nearby me are going through conflict, (in other words, not necessarily have demons or anything but are just going through a tough time) I feel it as a knot in my stomach. In fact, sometimes it's a bit unbelievable. I have this awful knot inside. What I am discerning is that somebody is going through a conflict.

When I feel this, I know it is time to pray for them or perhaps get in touch and see if they need ministry. More often than not, they had been going through a tough time and were asking the Lord for help. The Lord will manifest this gift in me to recognize the problem and be the answer to their prayer.

Perhaps you have already started functioning in some of this but didn't realize it. When you learn to flow in it I promise you, your personal as well as your public ministry, will never be the same again.

HOW THE PROPHET ROCKS THE GIFT OF DISCERNING OF SPIRITS

> *1 Corinthians 12:10 to another the working of miracles, to another prophecy, to another discerning of spirits, to another different kinds of tongues, to another the interpretation of tongues.*

Colette Toach

> *1 John 4:1 Beloved, do not believe every spirit, but test the spirits, whether they are of God; because many false prophets have gone out into the world.*
>
> *2 By this you know the Spirit of God: Every spirit that confesses that Jesus Christ has come in the flesh is of God,*
>
> *3 and every spirit that does not confess that Jesus Christ has come in the flesh is not of God. And this is the spirit of the Antichrist, which you have heard was coming, and is now already in the world.*

I have addressed many principles in these chapters on how to test the spirits and judge revelation, but at the end of the day, the one thing that will remain constant and will tell you the truth from a lie is the gift of discerning of spirits.

There will be times when even the principles I have covered here will not really help you identify a deception. The Word says that satan comes as an angel of light and at times a revelation can look and sound so right, but still not be of the Lord!

Consider this example:

> *Jeremiah 14:13 Then I said, "Ah, Lord God! Behold, the prophets say to them, 'You shall not see the sword, nor shall you have famine, but I will give you assured peace in this place.'"*
>
> *14 And the Lord said to me, "The prophets prophesy lies in My name. I have not sent them, commanded them, nor spoken to them; they prophesy to you a false vision, divination, a worthless thing, and the deceit of their heart."*

In this instant, the prophets seem to be prophesying faith, hope and love! They were telling the people that things would go well with them and that they would not see death, where Jeremiah was coming with a word of judgment! So how can you tell the difference?

It is the gift of discerning of spirits that will give you this revelation. For God can see the heart of man, and only He can clarify if a word is from Him or not, no matter how many principles you use to discern and to judge. It is only by the gift of discerning of spirits that you can truly judge a word.

If the prophets are to judge the spirit of the prophets, how else will you do it unless you operate in the gift of discerning of spirits? It could be that you have in fact been operating in this gift for some time, but just did not know it.

So let's look at the definition of this gift, how you can receive it and then finally how it will operate in your life and ministry.

1. DEFINITION

Firstly, if you take a quick look at the Strong's concordance for this passage, you will see exactly what this gift is. So for those who have a teaching orientation and love to dig into the "behind the scenes" details, you will enjoy this point.

Here is a copy of the passage I quoted at the beginning of this lesson including all of the Strong's numbers.

> 1 Corinthians 12:10 <1161> To another <243> the working <1755> of miracles <1411>; <1161> to another <243> prophecy <4394>; <1161> to another <243> **discerning <1253> of spirits <4151>**; <1161> to another <2087> divers kinds <1085> of tongues <1100>; <1161> to another <243> the interpretation <2058> of tongues <1100>:(KJV)

If you break that down, this is what you will find:

> **discerning <1253>**
> AV - discerning 1, discern 1, disputation 1; 3
>
> 1) a distinguishing, discerning, judging
>
> **of spirits <4151>; <1161>**
> AV - Spirit 111, Holy Ghost 89, Spirit (of God) 13,
>
> Spirit (of the Lord) 5, (My) Spirit 3, Spirit (of truth) 3,
>
> Spirit (of Christ) 2, human (spirit) 49, (evil) spirit 47,
>
> spirit (general) 26, spirit 8, (Jesus' own) spirit 6,
>
> (Jesus' own) ghost 2, misc 21; 385

The number behind each of these definitions lets you know how many times this Greek word was used in this way in the New Testament. So this Greek word was translated 111 times as Spirit, 89 times as Holy Ghost, 49 times as Human Spirit and so forth.

But if you take an overall look at these definitions you will see that the spirits that Paul is referring to here can speak of the Spirit of the Lord, a human spirit or even an evil/demonic spirit.

So to tie this all together, the gift of discerning of spirits is the ability to discern or distinguish the spirit or anointing of the Lord, the condition of a human spirit or the presence of a demon or oppression.

To have this gift gives you the ability to know when the anointing of God is on a person or a word, whether a person or a revelation is influenced by Satan and it will also give you the ability to sense a conflict of a human spirit and what is going on in their hearts.

Later on I will be teaching you how to differentiate between all of these, but for now let's just move on to receiving this gift and to using it!

2. RECEIVING IT

By now you should already know that all of the gifts are received through desire and by faith. If you desire this gift, you need to know that the day you got saved that the Holy Spirit came to dwell in you and brought all the gifts with Him!

Is He not the one that manifests Himself as He wills? You already have the potential within you! All you need to do is reach out by faith and ask the Holy Spirit to manifest Himself through this gift in your life!

If you would reach out in faith and desire and earnestly seek Him for it, He will give it to you! Either you will receive it by His hand, or He may lead you to receive it by impartation by another person. Either way if you ask, He will honor you and give it to you.

3. USING IT

Now you might already be functioning in this gift without knowing it! Just like I shared in my illustration in the book of my teacher and I coming to the same mathematical solution via a different route, so also will each prophet sense these things in different ways.

For some who operate in this gift, they smell either the presence of the Lord or the presence of a demon. They might smell the anointing as a fragrance of roses and the presence of a demon as tobacco or as something that is rotting.

Others will hear the presence of demons or angels. Yet the two most common ways are to see and to feel. You might be in prayer or in a church meeting and you will get a vision of an angel or a demon. If you are in personal ministry you might see a vision of the person that you are ministering to bound by chains.

This is the gift of discerning of spirits. The Holy Spirit is showing what is going on in the spirit and what to do.

Personally I feel the presence of a demon before I see him in the spirit. I feel it as goose bumps on my arms and on my head. Craig on the other hand, feels it in his hand like a tingling. Another shares how he experiences it as a pulling sensation in his hands. Now you might sense the presence of a demon or someone who is under oppression in a different way, but maybe you can already identify with the examples I have listed.

Now you would sense the anointing differently. I sense it as a warm glow or a feeling of being lifted up. I might see a vision of the glory of God, but more often I will feel the anointing of the Lord. It brings a peace and a soothing over my body and soul. You might feel the anointing in a different way.

Maybe when the anointing is present, you want to cry. I know that many people often feel the anointing in that way and we have often joked about it because we will sometimes come to deliver a prophetic word and the anointing will be so strong that we see many people brought to tears.

So learn to identify these things in your life. When you are in a meeting where the Lord is present, how do you feel? Now next time you feel that same thing when you speak to a person or listen to a song, you know that the Lord is there.

Then again, can you identify a time when you sensed the presence of a demon? Make a note of that because a time may come when someone comes to speak to you or even to give a prophetic word and you will feel this again. When you feel it, then you will know that they are under oppression and not to receive the word that they are speaking.

As you become more aware of the various ways that the Holy Spirit is speaking to you, you will develop these gifts and be a vessel that the Lord will be able to pick up and use any time that He wills!

This chapter was taken from the book **Prophetic Essentials** and the **Practical Prophetic Ministry Student Manual** written by Colette Toach.

SCRIPTURES TO MEMORIZE

1 John 4:1 Beloved, do not believe every spirit, but test the spirits, whether they are of God; because many false prophets have gone out into the world.

2 By this you know the Spirit of God: Every spirit that confesses that Jesus Christ has come in the flesh is of God,

3 and every spirit that does not confess that Jesus Christ has come in the flesh is not of God. And this is the spirit of the Antichrist, which you have heard was coming, and is now already in the world.

1 Corinthians 12:10 to another the working of miracles, to another prophecy, to another discerning of spirits, to another different kinds of tongues, to another the interpretation of tongues.

KEY PRINCIPLES

- ✓ The gift of discerning of spirits is the ability to discern the spiritual realm. The ability to discern or see the presence of angels and demons.
- ✓ It is also the ability to sense the condition of another human's spirit.
- ✓ It is only by the gift of discerning of spirits that you can truly judge a word.
- ✓ You receive the gift of discerning of spirits by faith.

PRACTICAL APPLICATION

1. **MAKE A NOTE OF THE FOLLOWING EVENTS:**

    a. Make a note of the last five meetings you attended.

    _____
    _____
    _____
    _____
    _____

    b. Make a note of the last time you ministered to someone.

    _____
    _____
    _____

    c. Make a note of the last time you listened to or watched a teaching.

    _____
    _____
    _____
    _____

d. Make a note of the last time you received ministry.

___

2. **NOW UNDER EACH ONE OF THOSE EVENTS, MAKE THE FOLLOWING OBSERVATIONS:**

   a. What emotions did I feel in this event?

___

b. What did I feel deep down in my spirit during this event?

___

c. What visions did I receive during these times?

___

d. Did I feel something positive or negative during this time?

EXTRA NOTES:

Chapter 03

Dealing with Demons and Deception

Chapter 03 – Dealing with Demons and Deception

Chapter Reference: *The Minister's Handbook*, Chapter 9

Nobody likes to talk about deception and out of all the fivefold ministry - prophets are about the worst! I have found that a prophet (especially in training) would rather die than admit that his revelation was not from the Lord.

I do not know what the hang up is about. Sure deception is not very pleasant, but it is a vital part of the training God takes His ministers through. In fact, it is so vital that you will not be able to pass through your ministry training properly without going through the "deception phase."

This is no different with someone called to the teaching ministry. It is only when they have tried to get revelation in the flesh and failed, that they will recognize truth when it really comes. It is only when you have failed and fallen for the honeyed words of the enemy can you be armed with a true understanding of heresy and how it can come about in the first place.

All of us have moments of the flesh and I am here to reassure you by saying that it is part of the process. In fact, it is vital to the process of being able to identify deception and the work of the enemy in others.

As in all things, you have to live it for yourself first before qualifying to point it out in others later.

It takes someone who has matured in the Lord to say, "I missed it!" As I have worked with many leaders, I get so many different kinds of people at different places in their training.

However, when I come across someone who is not afraid to say, "Oops! I missed it! I failed there!" I know that I am working with someone who has matured in the Lord.

So I am going to ask something strangely ridiculous of you. I am going to ask you to get excited about the subject of deception. Now before you think I am crazy, hear me out for a bit. When you finally stand up and speak God's word and you can do so with confidence, knowing that you are speaking exactly what you should, it brings such a rest.

Let us not be naïve and think, "All my revelations are pure and come directly from the Throne Room of God and should be taken word for word as such."

My advice? Grow up a little bit. Let's be honest, we are not perfect. We can mess things up. Now if you can be humble and admit that you are able to be deceived you will have a good chance of not being deceived.

If you think that you cannot get into deception, then you already are!

A good place to be is admitting that you can fail and get into deception. From there, you can realize that it is all right to fail! If you have been in deception in the past, I would never condemn you for it. I would judge you however if you did get into deception and you are not prepared to face and deal with it.

PLAY IT SAFE

So here are some good points to help you to clear up what is deception and what is not. While I point these out to you, it's just you and these pages, so be open. Do not read through the points and say to yourself, "Yup! I can think of a few people who need to read this!"

Instead point a good straight finger at yourself and face your fears right here and now. If you are prepared to do that here in the quiet of your room, then you will not have to face the humiliation of any startling discoveries of deception later in public!

I cannot think of anything more devastating than a prophet that refuses to look at the truth when it comes to deception. They would rather hold onto their false revelation because of the recognition they get, than to know the reality of Jesus Christ.

Why settle for second best? So let's look at this subject openly. No holds barred. You are welcome to pull out some of your revelations from the past and have a good, honest look at where you stand. No one is condemning or judging you. This is solely between you and the Lord.

THE SPIRIT OF DIVINATION

You will find this kind of deception referenced to a lot in both the New and Old Testaments. You would be shocked if you knew how much of this is rampant in the Church right now.

It is not uncommon for someone to come to us, interested in our prophetic training saying, "You know ever since I was a child I used to dream of bad things happening and then they would come to pass. Now I realize I was just a prophet all along!

I thought I was strange back then, but now I realize I had a prophetic gift and that it was God showing me these things!"

I look at them and think, "No... it was not because of a prophetic calling, you are in fact demonized!"

That is not how the Holy Spirit works, that is the work of a demon.

It is no different to the fortuneteller that ran after Paul saying, "Listen to them, because they have been sent by the most high." We all know how Paul handled that, don't we? He turned around and rebuked that demon and told it to leave her.

After that she did not do any fortune telling. That is what the spirit of divination looks like. I find people who have this kind of bondage the hardest to deal with.

The reason is because they think that the voice that they are hearing and the visions that they are receiving are really from the Lord.

A TRUE STORY

There was a Christian woman that wrote in to me once. She said that she had certain experiences where she would experience things before they happened. She told me one of her experiences where she heard a voice tell her that her father was going to die and then it went on to even give the date and time.

And so she lived in constant fear as she approached this date. As the time came closer the fateful day arrived and in the morning everything seemed all right. However, that evening they got a knock at the door saying that her father had disappeared and that they did not know where he had gone.

So she prayed and suddenly she got a revelation and knew exactly where he was. So they rushed to him and found him trying to commit suicide. She grabbed him and he seemed to be suddenly shaken. As if coming out of a dream, he looked at her and said, "You know, I do not know what came over me, I just suddenly wanted to commit suicide."

That is not the work of the Holy Spirit! The worst part is that she sent this as a testimony saying, "I must be a prophet because I knew that before it happened." No, she did not "know" that this was going to happen.

The sad truth is that she released it by believing that demonic word. She gave satan license to do exactly what he wanted to do. The difficult truth is that she could have brought about the death of her father. That is scary, but it is the cold truth about the spirit of divination.

If the enemy can get a hold in your life and through his spirit of divination give you revelations, as you speak them out and have faith in them, you release them to come to pass in the earth. You give satan the exact license that he wanted to work out his own plan.

That is why the spirit of divination is deadly. So do not think that just because you knew something was going to happen and it did, that it was God speaking. We do not serve a Savior of strife, fear and condemnation.

The Lord does not go around telling you that people will be murdered and destroyed. If you know Jesus as I know Jesus, you will know that He does not operate in that way. You would know that Jesus brings faith, hope and love through everything He tells us.

His words do not produce fear or condemnation.

I consider the passage where Jesus spoke to Peter about the way he would die. He told Peter that when he was an old man, that he would be led to a place he did not want to go. (John 21:18) This revelation did not bring fear to Peter.

In fact, some time later Peter was bound and put in prison. There was talk of death and punishment, yet when the angel came to save him, he had to give Peter a kick to wake him up. Could you fall into a nice comfy sleep knowing that this could be your last night on earth?

You see, Peter knew that this was not his last night on earth. In fact, he knew that he would be a nice old man before he would have to die, so he could sleep peacefully. This revelation gave Peter hope. It did not bring fear and it also did not come with graphic detail. It only gave an indication.

This is another big difference I see with a spirit of divination. The images are usually very vivid and clear, whereas the Lord always speaks in types and shadows. History tells us that Peter was crucified upside down, but this is not what Jesus told him.

Instead He said to him, "Another will dress you and lead you to a place you do not want to go… "Can you see the difference here between this and the encounter I shared before it?

ALL IS NOT LOST

Now as you read this and you suspect that you have had similar experiences that hint towards a spirit of divination, I want to say that all is not lost. You can be set free and come to hear the voice of the Lord clearly.

I must be blatantly honest with you though and say that if you suspect a spirit of divination in your life, then there is a demon involved. There is something strongly demonic that is binding you and holding you back. It is blocking you from a face-to-face relationship with Jesus.

That horrible demon is destroying what God is trying to do in your life. In fact, it could well be that a lot of the problems and struggles you have been facing in life have not just been prophetic preparation. All those tough times might very well be the result of that bondage in your life.

Now if this is speaking to you, now is not the time to allow yourself to get under condemnation or to try and justify yourself. You need to rise up and shake this thing off!

You have authority in the name of Jesus to deal with this. It is best if you have someone who can stand in agreement with you, but if you do not, you can still take authority over it on your own.

DEALING WITH IT

> *James 4:7* *Therefore submit to God. Resist the devil and he will flee from you.*

So the first thing that you need to do is acknowledge your sin. Satan did not jump in when you were not looking. He may have given you the deception, but you received and believed it. You took it into your heart.

So the first step is to ask the Lord for forgiveness for allowing that thing a hold in your life. This might even be something that has been passed down through your generations. You might see it in your family as well and you grew up with it your whole life. You still gave it license.

There was a time in your life when you gave it a place in your heart and you need to repent of that and submit yourself to the Lord once again.

I hope that what I am stirring up in you is a righteous anger, because you do not have to accept this deception. You do not need to take whatever the enemy dishes out. You can enter into a new relationship with Jesus!

Once you have submitted, then you can resist and tell that demon to take a hike. You can command it to stop its influence over you.

UNDERSTANDING STRANGE EXPERIENCES

Perhaps as I have shared, you can identify with a few of these experiences, but it is not typically a habit in your life. What I want you to do is think back on these experiences and think about what was happening with you at the time.

Identify the circumstances you were in at the time this strange experience occurred. Perhaps you had a mentor or were going to a specific church at that time. Did you perhaps get involved in a new teaching or did someone lay hands on you and impart something to you?

The point is that during this time you opened your heart to something that was not of the Lord. You received something here that gave the enemy license in your life. Once you can identify it, you can quickly submit to the Lord and see the enemy for what he truly is.

You can turn around and tell the enemy that his number is up! You will not listen to his voice any longer. You have authority in the name of Jesus. You are not a victim and you can overcome this thing.

THERE IS A GOOD SIDE

Although having to look at divination in your life does not sound like a lot of fun, there is a good side to it. Once you have overcome it, you will be able to identify it so much easier in others. So break free and then teach them to break free.

If you have not had these experiences for yourself, I promise that you will come across people that have and you better know how to minister to them. Do not mistake their "gift" for prophetic ministry. Above all do not feel insecure next to someone who has those strange experiences.

DO NOT FEEL INSECURE!

When a person is under the influence of a spirit of divination, their "revelations" sound so out of this world. There is a temptation to feel insecure next to that. You think, "Well I just want to speak a word of encouragement so that I can bring people into a relationship with Jesus. I do not run around having out of body experiences."

You know what? You are the one that has the truth. Never feel insecure about that!

HOW DECEPTION COMES

Deception is different to the spirit of divination. Divination is akin to witchcraft whereas deception is simply a revelation that was not from God.

It comes a bit like this:

You received this incredible revelation from the Lord for someone. So you rushed up to them and gushed all over them! Instead of being impressed, they look at you as if you just crawled out of a piece of cheese.

You wanted to crawl away. You thought to yourself, "What happened there? What was that?"

The answer: It was just deception.

You will identify deception by the pushiness that comes with it. Now here are a few things that you need to watch out for. Deception is identified in a word that brings fear to the hearer instead of love. It sounds a bit like,

"You better come right with God or He is going to take your son away from you."

"You better repent or God is going to destroy your business."

That is not the spirit of Christ. That is deception. It is a revelation that did not come from the Lord, but from the enemy. Once again (sorry to break it to you) but you are not a victim.

If you are receiving revelations that are a deception, then something is wrong. There could be a number of reasons why you missed it. It could be that you are not under spiritual authority.

WHERE DID IT COME FROM?

If you suspect that you have fallen into deception, identifying where you opened the door to the enemy is a huge leap forward. Look for any strange teachings you got into, mentors that you received from in the past or perhaps others that spoke into your life that were in deception.

It could be that you received from someone that was not under any kind of authority or covering from a team themselves and some of their revelations and experiences felt a bit strange to you. Before opening up and just taking everything from someone, see if the spirit they are walking in is of the Lord.

You can identify the fruit of a prophet by the trail of disaster or the blessing that they leave behind. Now I am not saying that every revelation that we speak should be all pretty and nice.

CONDEMNATION VS. CONVICTION

Sure, there are times when the Lord will call on you to speak a word of warning. There will be times when you will speak with a strong conviction and anointing. However, even though you might be issuing a correction or warning, that word should bring a conviction.

It should bring the person to their knees before the Lord. It should not leave them trembling in fear or guilt.

> ***2 Corinthians 7:10*** *For godly sorrow produces repentance leading to salvation, not to be regretted; but the sorrow of the world produces death.*

If you bring a word that produces condemnation, it only brings death. You leave the person thinking, "What is the point of going on any longer? I give up. What is the use of serving the Lord?"

This is the sorrow of the world - it is not conviction. When you speak a word of correction and they are pierced in their hearts and fall before the Lord, you can rest assured that you are speaking on behalf of the King of kings.

Their relationship with God is restored and when you see this happen, the short sorrow they might experience because of the correction is short lived. They do not regret it, because it did something wonderful in their lives. That is why it says that true godly sorrow comes without regret.

You never regret a good conviction. I personally love a good conviction. One of those when the Holy Spirit speaks so clearly and it cuts you straight to the heart. You feel so naked before the Lord and you fall flat on your face and cry before Him.

It is a good experience because you get up again feeling so cleansed and closer to the Lord. So do not confuse condemnation and conviction.

DO IT NOW!

Many of us have experienced this one at one time or another. You are sitting in the meeting and you feel that you must give the word that God has given to you *right now*! If you do not give the word, then you have failed God and their blood is on your hands.

So you stand up and say, "The Lord is going to destroy this church because you refuse to repent." Then you sit down and you feel a sinking feeling in the pit of your stomach.

That pushiness you felt was not of the Lord. The Lord Jesus is a gentleman and He leads. He does not push and shove. The Scripture refers to the Holy Spirit as a dove and the Lord Jesus as a shepherd.

When last did you see a shepherd standing behind the sheep with a stick, whacking them from behind and telling them to move their fluffy little tails?

No, the Good Shepherd goes ahead of the sheep and leads them. Even when a sheep goes astray and He has to pull that sheep from the pit with his staff, it might be uncomfortable, but it is to save its life.

The worst with that pushy feeling is when you were not sure, so you did not stand up and give the word. Afterwards though you feel just terrible and you think you failed the Lord. The Lord will never make you feel guilty because you did not let Him use you.

There are many others that He can use. You do not hold the world in your hand, He does. He is well able to raise up many others to speak His word.

So do not allow yourself to come under that condemnation. If you think back and feel that horrible guilty feeling, then I want you to let it go right now. The Lord does not condemn you and the guilt is not from Him. That is the voice of the enemy accusing you.

BEING PUSHED BEYOND WHAT GOD INTENDS

I remember when I learned this lesson for myself. I learned that when the enemy cannot get away with deceiving you, then he will push you beyond what God intends. In other words, the enemy will take something that is real and he will push you to the point where you will start off with a real revelation and take it way beyond what you were meant to.

EXAMPLE

Say for example you are attending a church where the pastor often uses tithing to keep the people in bondage. The deacons that have been appointed gave a lot of money to the church and you wonder how much of their appointment had to do with calling or the size of their check.

The ones who are promoted are the ones who give the most, while those who have a real anointing are not given a chance.

Your heart burns for change. And so as you are interceding the Lord gives you a revelation. He says that He is going to start leading the church in a new direction and do something that He has never done there before.

He is going to open doors that will change the way they have been going and that He is going to lead them to a new land.

This is a fantastic word, but unfortunately with all your frustration of "the system" in this church, instead of sharing it like that, you share it differently.

You stand up and say to the pastor, "God has seen what you are doing and He is going to bring about a change in this church. He is going to force you to go His way and not to follow your own way any longer.

And if you do not follow His way, He will break this foundation and break this church down that you have built."

What just happened here? You were just pushed beyond what God intended! That is not what the Lord meant, but because of your own anger, when that word came out of you it did not come as it should have.

This is something that you will have to watch out the most for as a minister.

PRE-CONCEIVED IDEAS

It is just so easy to look at someone from the outside and to assess them, knowing that they have a problem in their lives. You might even know that they are bitter towards you.

As you are praying with them, you get a revelation and instead of "saying it like it is" you try to interpret it to deal with their bitterness against you. You will not minister to their need, but you will add to that revelation.

When you are aware of this in yourself, you will see it in others that stand up to minister. It is humbling when the Lord reveals this in you because you realize that although you had some zeal, you did not represent Christ.

AVOIDING DECEPTION

STOP!

When you are ministering to someone that you are struggling to love or you feel too much emotion regarding a church or person, it would do you good to stop and wait for a confirmation or to journal your revelation first.

Wait for your emotions to calm down and be sure that you are speaking in faith, hope and love. I have said this a hundred times before and will probably say it a hundred times more - Err on the side of speaking blessing.

You can never go wrong by speaking blessing. Speaking a blessing does not bring harm to anyone, however speaking a curse can bring about devastating results. So if the word you feel you must bring is one of correction or judgment, you better be pretty sure that the correction is coming from the Lord and not your own pre-conceived ideas.

If you come with the right attitude, it will bring conviction and there will be change. Make sure that when you stand up to minister, that the vision or word you share is of God, as well as the interpretation.

A WORD TO THE LADIES

Women do not like me saying this, but I am going to say it anyway because I just so happen to be one myself, so I can get away with it. Ladies, you have to be under the submission of your husbands. The Scripture is clear. Adam came before Eve, because Eve missed it badly.

The Lord has given us our husbands to cover and protect us. Run to your husband and come under his protection. Do not run off on your own and try to run the ministry all by yourself. If you do that, you are begging to get into deception.

If you are an unmarried woman, then find yourself a spiritual father.

This is certainly the stand in our ministry. None of us are loners. We all work within a team so that we can cover one another. Even though Craig and I stand in apostolic office, we do not run off independently and do what we want, when we want. We cover one another's backs.

TWO BY TWO

The enemy will certainly try to sneak in. Even Jesus sent His disciples out two by two. Even after Jesus was glorified, everyone traveled as a team.

Apostle Paul traveled with Luke, Timothy and Silas. Even Peter traveled with his wife doing the work of the ministry. If Jesus did it and the apostles did it, is this not our example to follow? No one is meant to be an island and to do things alone.

I do not like being negative, but have someone there to watch your back. If you try to head out into the great blue yonder all alone and you fall flat on your face, there is nothing worse than falling alone. Not only that, but if you have someone else there to cover you, you have less of a chance of hitting that big wall in front of you that reads, "NOT THIS WAY!"

So even if you are a man, realize that God has called you to work in a team setting. Do not run off and make major decisions without getting backing from your team. Learn to be a team player and this will help prevent you from getting into deception.

KNOW YOUR LIMITATIONS

It is good to know your weaknesses and limitations. I had to correct someone for an incorrect dream interpretation once and instead of being open enough to listen she said, "I only speak when God tells me to speak. I only prophesy what God tells me to prophesy. This ministry is not of God and is a complete deception and I want nothing to do with you, because I only speak what God tells me to."

She then went on to slander us with some terrible insults that were not only personal, but also very incorrect!

I thought to myself, "Not only are you arrogant, but you are deceived to think that you only speak what God tells you, when right there, the voice coming from her was anything but the voice of the Lord Jesus Christ."

Be a little mature and be prepared to look at yourself and to admit that maybe... just maybe, not everything you speak is what God is really speaking.

If you have that kind of humility and you are open to correction, then the Holy Spirit can train you so much quicker. However, if you say, "I am only here to minister. I only give the words when God says and I press on forward and never give up. God can count on me because I am so humble. You have never seen anyone more humble than me."

That is so self-righteous and someone like that is like a hard rock that God has to smash before any real training can begin.

Rather say, "Ok Lord, I am open. Show me! Where did I miss it?"

Now you are ready! Now you are mature and the Lord can start working with you and training you. Sure, it is not so comfortable.

It is not fun to mess up! But you know I have greater respect for someone who messes up and then takes responsibility saying, "Yes! I failed." Than I do for someone who goes off on a tangent all the time and is never prepared to admit that maybe they are not perfect.

What can God do with such a person? I look at King David and he was so humble. You read his Psalms and you see how he was not afraid to speak out all of his failures and mistakes. He was not afraid to voice his fears, but yet he was the greatest king that Israel ever had.

DO NOT BE AFRAID TO BE HUMBLE

God can do something with someone who is prepared to be humble. Then with all of your failure and weakness, you will certainly rise up higher than those who put on the mask of superiority. I would rather hang out with someone who is real than with someone who wears a mask and that you cannot get close to.

SIGNS OF DECEPTION

We have covered this in many places, so I am going to make this easy for you and list just 5 clear signs of deception for you to remember and to weigh your revelations with.

Pull out some of your own revelations and compare them. Then look around at some of the revelations others are sharing and weigh them as well.

SIGN 1: IT DOES NOT LINE UP WITH THE WORD

This might seem obvious to you, but you will still see many saying, "This is what God is telling you…" when the Word tells us the complete opposite.

I had a woman come to me confused and frustrated. She was going through a bad time in her marriage and she and her husband were in continual conflict. He was a Christian. She came and said that she had received a prophetic word that she was to divorce her husband and to move on.

Clearly this word is not from God. The Lord is not in the business of telling people to get divorced, without first following the clear guidelines in the Word.

SIGN 2: THE WORD BRINGS FEAR

The scripture says that the spirit that has been given is not of fear, but of a sound mind. If you are bringing fear that completely disables a person, something is wrong. Now I am not talking about a reverential fear of the Lord, but the kind of fear that brings death.

An example is a woman preacher who told two men who did not want to get saved that the Lord was going to kill them because of it. This is not the voice of the Lord Jesus. How do I know this? Because Jesus Himself said he did not come to the world to judge it, but to save it from its sins. Jesus died for us to save us. He did not come to save us… only to kill us later on down the line!

SIGN 3: THE WORD BRINGS GUILT AND CONDEMNATION

This kind of word can bring a lot of confusion as well. Someone might come into a meeting feeling on top of the world, but they leave it under such guilt that they feel they cannot come to the Lord any longer.

They leave feeling as if they failed the Lord and are not worthy to come into His presence. They look as if they are walking under a load. This is the kind of thing that Jesus accused the Pharisees of all the time. He said that they weighed the people down with such a load and then never lifted a finger to help them carry it.

SIGN 4: WATCH THE PUSHINESS!

If you feel that you have to "drop everything" and give the word immediately, then be careful. The Lord does not push - He leads. If you feel the sudden urge to run and force your revelation, wait on it for a bit.

You might be doing a chore in your house when suddenly a revelation comes out of nowhere and you feel the urge to drop everything and act on it right now! Wait on that word or impulse and give the Holy Spirit time to confirm it for you. I have found in personal experience that when you wait on the word a bit that if it was not of the Lord, the feeling often fades. However, the words that are truly from God are confirmed through others and through the Scriptures later on.

SIGN 5: WHEN THE WORD EXALTS THE PERSON

Unfortunately, we see this way too often. People leave a meeting saying, "Wow! That man was so amazing. He saw that great demon and then he spoke to that angel. Then, he had such an incredible revelation. He must be so close to God. Wow! I wish I was like him!"

People leave that meeting speaking about that man and how wonderful he is and the Lord Jesus is... where? Did this ministry bring the people closer to the Lord or did it bring the people closer to the prophet?

Watch out for that. Now I am not saying that God does not give great revelations, because He sure can. I am talking of people that walk in that all of the time, sharing their great experiences more than they share about our great God.

Is the point of ministry not to glorify the Lord? It is Christ in us that is the hope of glory and it is through our weakness where His strength is displayed.

When we stand up with this kind of attitude, it ministers Christ to the people and draws them into a relationship with Him.

No one should leave a meeting that you ministered at thinking that God forgot about them. They should not leave thinking that you are more important to God than what they are. They should leave with hope that they too can have a relationship with Jesus and that He cares about every part of their lives.

Hopefully by now you understand deception a little bit and that the mystery is gone. Everyone that has been in ministry has experienced one

Spiritual Discernment Workshop

of these shortcomings at one time or another. So do not be discouraged if you too fell for one of the tricks of the enemy.

Rather submit yourself to the Lord, resist the devil and he will flee from you. (James 4:7). Then rise up once again in your authority, knowing that what the enemy sought for evil, God has the power to turn around for His good.

This chapter was taken from the *Minister's Handbook* written by Colette Toach.

SCRIPTURES TO MEMORIZE

James 4:7 *Therefore submit to God. Resist the devil and he will flee from you.*

2 Corinthians 7:10 *For godly sorrow produces repentance leading to salvation, not to be regretted; but the sorrow of the world produces death.*

KEY PRINCIPLES

- ✓ Deception it is a vital part of the training God takes His ministers through.
- ✓ The number 1 sign of deception is that the revelation doesn't line up with the Word of God.
- ✓ A word that is not of the Lord brings forth fear, guilt, condemnation, strife and division.
- ✓ Divination is akin to witchcraft whereas deception is simply a revelation that was not from God.
- ✓ A godly warning or correction brings conviction and not condemnation.

PRACTICAL APPLICATION:

1. **HAVE YOU EVER EXPERIENCED THAT "PUSHINESS" IN MINISTRY? HAS THIS OCCURRED MORE THAN ONCE?**

_____

_____

_____

_____

_____

_____

2. **DOCUMENT A TIME WHEN YOU FELT A STRONG FEAR TO MINISTER.**

   "I must do this now or else..."

3. **HAVE YOU EVER SEEN SOMEONE IN DECEPTION? GIVE DETAILS.**

4. **WHAT FEARS OR CONCERNS DO YOU HAVE CONCERNING THE DEMONIC AND DEMONIC MANIFESTATIONS?**

_____

_____

_____

_____

_____

5. **LOOKING BACK, HAVE YOU EVER NEEDED TO DEAL WITH OR SEEN A DEMONIC MANIFESTATION IN SOMEONE?**

_____

_____

_____

_____

   a. What was the outcome?

_____

_____

_____

_____

_____

b. If the outcome was bad, using the points in the book, what was done incorrectly?

_____

_____

_____

_____

_____

_____

c. If the outcome was good, using the principles in the book, what could have been added?

_____

_____

_____

_____

_____

_____

EXTRA NOTES

CHAPTER 04

DEALING WITH DEMONIC MANIFESTATIONS

Chapter 04 – Dealing with Demonic Manifestations

Chapter Reference: *The Minister's Handbook*, Chapter 10

No one ever forgets the first time that a demon manifests during their ministry. Suddenly all of the principles that you have learned seemed to fly out your head as you face the reality of dealing with a demon face to face.

The first times for Craig and I was just as startling. We were holding a home church meeting when during praise and worship, a woman started manifesting a demon and shouting at us. Her voice changed, her eyes changed and it was clear that when you looked at her face, she was no longer in control of her senses.

So we made the first mistake everyone usually makes. We told the demon to get out. It did not. We shouted. The demon shouted. We shouted louder. The demon shouted louder. Clearly we were not getting anywhere.

She was only getting more violent and for a moment she launched at me, stopping an inch from my face. In that moment I felt such a peace of the Lord come over me. I knew this enemy and I knew that he was defeated 2000 years ago. I looked the woman straight in the face and I called her by name.

I did not talk to the demon. He was really not worthy of my time. It was the woman I wanted to help out here and as I looked at her, I felt a deep compassion for her. The demon stopped short, just staring at me with a bewildered look on its face.

Then I reached out, took the woman's hand and said, "Hey, I love you, the Lord Jesus loves you and we want to help you break free here."

The demon gave me one more confused look and then the woman's face changed as she returned to her senses. After that we could counsel her and get her to renounce the hold the enemy had on her.

We had another similar experience in a public meeting. As I was leading praise and worship a woman started manifesting a demon at the back of the meeting hall. Dressed from head to toe in a classy white suit, she was yelling and rolling on the dusty wooden floor from one end to the other.

Craig walked politely up to the woman, tapped her on the shoulder and said, "Could you come with us please." He did not argue and he did not try to "fight it out" with the demon right there. Instead he spoke to the woman.

Together with another minister he took her aside and they could minister to her and help her break free. She had experienced this manifestation for many years and thought that it was the power of the Holy Spirit throwing her all over the floor all these years.

Not only was this manifestation an interruption to the meeting every time the anointing began to flow, but it was a blockage in this woman's life. She always came so far in her walk with God and no further. She could not understand what that blockage was. Once they showed her in the Word the kind of gentleman Jesus was, she was ready to renounce that bondage.

No further demonic manifestations were needed. She submitted herself to God, repented of her sin and told the enemy to leave. The manifestations did not return and she made the first real steps forward in her spiritual growth.

TWO CAMPS

The reason I have shared a few of our own examples is to bring some balance between two main camps in the church when it comes to demonic manifestations. You have some who are just "too afraid" to go there and avoid the demonic realm altogether.

Then on the other end of the pendulum you find "deliverance ministries" who see demons everywhere that they go.

Yes, demons are real. Yes, angels are real. However, never forget:

> ***Philippians 2:10*** *that at the name of Jesus every knee should bow, of those in heaven, and of those on earth, and of those under the earth.*

> ***Luke 10:19*** *Behold, I give you the authority to trample on serpents and scorpions, and over all the power of the enemy, and nothing shall by any means hurt you.*

I cover a lot of detail regarding the doctrine of demons and angels in *Prophetic Warrior*, but I will mention one point here that is poignant. If you do a study, you will notice that the Apostles did not go around casting demons out of believers.

You see the work of Jesus and He often cast demons out of people, but this was before he was crucified. These people were not born again and this kind of deliverance was not restricted to Israelites either. He cast demons out of Israelites (Mary) and He cast demons out of the Syrophenician's daughter.

However, in the New Testament even though it was clear that Simon the Sorcerer was demonized, Peter did not "do deliverance" on the man. Rather he said, "You do not know the spirit you are of! I sense bitterness in you. You need to repent." (Acts 8)

This comes back to the point I made earlier in our counseling section of this book. There are times when you will have demon manifestations that you have to deal with right away. Then there are instances where the demon has gained entrance through hurts from the past or bitterness that the person has held onto.

While this is an extensive subject, I am going to give you some simple steps to follow on how to handle both of these situations.

DEMON MANIFESTATIONS

1. KNOW YOUR AUTHORITY

I am going to let you in on a secret here. Demons are not walking around just "jumping" into people. If someone is demonized, then they gave that demon license. Is this not true of your salvation? The Lord says that He stands at the door and knocks.

When you were born again, the Holy Spirit did not just overpower you and enter into your spirit without your free will, did He? No, the Lord has set up this earth and our lives with clear rules and guidelines. It was for Eve to choose to obey satan or not.

The moment that she obeyed satan and ate the fruit that she was not supposed to, she gave him license into this world. As a result, a curse entered into the earth. Adam and Eve lost their freedom and instead of walking in the blessing that God had given, they lost it.

Satan stole it, because they gave him that license in this earth. When God placed Adam into the garden, He gave him authority to tend it. Adam had the reins. He had the keys to lock and unlock. Unfortunately, though when they fell into sin, they handed that license over to the enemy.

Suddenly sin became an issue and that nasty little "seed of sin" entered into the world. That is a doctrinal study all on its own, but the greatest part of all is that the Lord did not leave it there. Right at that point the Lord said to them that He would send a Seed of His own through Eve that would crush the head of that serpent!

That seed was Jesus and through His blood we can now take back the authority that was lost to man in the Garden.

Not only does it make you appreciate your salvation all over again, but it also makes you realize that you have authority in the name of Jesus!

> **John 1:5** *And the light shineth in darkness, and the darkness comprehended it not. (KJV)*

I will never forget the look of confusion on that demon's face when I reached out to that woman in love. It is true that satan cannot understand love. It is completely contrary to his nature. It is as confusing as light is to darkness just like the scripture says above.

When your intent is to minister and help set someone free, you do not need to worry if you have the authority or the faith. This is a situation where your love will draw on the power of God to give you the gift of faith that you need.

2. TALK TO THE PERSON

It looks pretty awe-inspiring to see someone slithering around under demonic manifestation while the itinerant minister barks out commands and communicates with the demon.

Now let me ask you this question. If you were the person slithering around on the floor, how would you feel? When someone comes to me with an intimate problem, I counsel them privately and help them break free. As a counselor they trust me to bare their hearts and even share their sin so that I can help.

So how does this differ when it comes to demon manifestations? If someone does happen to manifest when you are ministering to them, you are not going to make any progress until you can get that person to be in agreement with you.

It is like I said before. If there is a demon, then that person gave it license through sin or direct demonic involvement. This could be through false religion, getting into heresy or even receiving an impartation from someone who was also bound.

This is when you take Peter's approach when dealing with Simon the Sorcerer. He spoke to Simon, not to the demon he obviously had. In the same way, if someone manifests, avoid the urge to struggle it out with the demon.

That demon has been given license in that person's life and he knows it. Your goal is to "cool down" that manifestation and to get that person in their right mind long enough to be able to help them break free.

Look at the person directly and call them by name. Ignore the demon and talk to the person sitting in front of you. Talk in love and wait for them to regain their control. Rest assured that even if the demon is going off like crazy that the person can hear you and that they can choose to take control again.

Never forget that they have the Holy Spirit inside of them and that they can break free.

NOTE: The only time this differs is if the person is an unbeliever. In the case of an unbeliever you can tell the demon to leave. When it leaves, it is important that you follow through with salvation or you stand the chance of them reverting once again.

DEMONS IN BELIEVERS VS. UNBELIEVERS

My dad shares an illustration between the difference of someone who is demonized who is a believer and someone who is not. He shares a story where a believer who was demonized had a standoff with a warlock.

While they both manifested a demon, there was one part of their experience that was decidedly different. The unbeliever could not remember everything that happened during the time the demon manifested. It was as if they had "blacked out".

The believer however could remember everything. They said that it was like standing and watching themselves say and do things, although they knew it was not really them doing it.

What makes the difference here is that a believer has the indwelling of the Holy Spirit. Remember the parable Jesus shared about the man who was set free of a demon? He said that the house is swept and made clean, but if that demon returns and finds it unoccupied, he brings back seven other demons and the man will be in a worse condition than before.

What Jesus was saying is, that it is not just good enough to go around casting out demons. The person also needs to get their "house" occupied. In other words, they need to get saved and have the Holy Spirit come and dwell inside of them.

When the Holy Spirit comes to dwell inside of you, He takes up permanent residence! Satan cannot control your spirit any longer. What he can do however is control your soul and this is what he will use in a believer. He will manipulate your mind, emotions and your will until he is told to leave.

When you understand these main points, you are ready to help set that person free.

3. BRING TRUE DELIVERANCE

Once the person has calmed down it is for you to bring conviction of sin. Just because someone manifested a demon does not mean they want to get rid of it. I just shared how satan takes control of the mind, emotions and will and this is where he plays his game.

Not only does he control this person, but he gives something to them as well. Perhaps the person in question is very insecure and unsure of themselves. This demonic force may give them the boldness that they lack. So it is not always a case of "casting out demons."

If you have seen someone set free of a demonic bondage only to regress again, this is the main reason why. The enemy's license was not removed. That person liked his demon. It sounds crazy hey? You only have to be in ministry for a short time to see the truth of this point.

This is why the Word of God is vital in this situation. A conviction of sin must come and that means relying on the Holy Spirit to bring that conviction. It is for you to allow them to see that they have sinned against God and as a result satan has a hold on their lives.

No matter how much they are benefitting from this demon, it is stealing their ability to rise up. Only when they are ready to look at their sin, can you progress to the steps I have mentioned below.

SETTING SOMEONE FREE

STEP 1: IDENTIFY THE OPEN DOOR

Like I said before demons do not go around just jumping into people. They have been given license through sin. Either that license came through family generations or through their own involvement. In many cases the open door will be clear.

If the person has used drugs or gotten involved in false religion, this is certainly a good place to start. In many countries witchcraft is a part of growing up. When ministering in places like this it can be really difficult.

We had a gentleman attend one of our conferences and ask for prayer. He had experienced out of body experiences since he was a child and he needed to know if these things were of God. God was starting to move him into the prophetic ministry and he was suddenly uncomfortable with all these strange experiences he kept having.

When we asked him when they started he said they were with him from birth. He went on to share that his parents were into voodoo and raised him in this until he got saved. That open door was pretty obvious. We told him that these manifestations were definitely not from the Holy Spirit. How could they be? He did not even have the indwelling of the Holy Spirit when he experienced it for the first time!

He was keen to deal with it and break free. No demon manifestations were necessary. He told it to leave and it left.

Some situations are not so clear. What does help is to ask the person when they first started experiencing these manifestations in their lives. It will usually come down to a specific time when they received something or got into something.

Once you know where the enemy got in, you are well on your way to victory.

STEP 2: REPENTANCE

James 4:7 says to submit yourself to God, resist the devil and he will flee. You cannot tell the enemy to go without submitting to God first. You disobeyed the Word of God through sin and you need to get right with God before you will have the authority to break free.

Jesus does not condemn you for your sin. He came to save you from it. However, the enemy is not as congenial. If he can take out a believer, he will use any means that he can.

So restore your relationship with the Lord first. The Word says that if our hearts do not condemn us, that we can approach the throne with boldness. You cannot break free if your heart condemns you. So lay the sin aside.

Repent of doing what you did or going where you went. In the case of generational bondages, break those generational links!

Daniel was a prime example of one who prayed on behalf of his people's sins. You can do the same regarding generational curses. You can repent for accepting whatever curse or bondage you allowed into your life. Once you have set things right with God, the most important thing is to tell the demon to leave.

STEP 3: DELIVERANCE

The scripture says that we have been given authority over serpents. Every believer has this authority, not just certain ministers. This means that the person in front of you has all the license and authority he needs to tell the demon to leave.

It was them who invited the demon through their sin - they have the same authority to take away that license. This is such a powerful step for anyone.

It is one thing to repent, but another to tell the devil to leave. When someone gets born again they make a choice to accept Jesus and to put off the old man so that he can put on the new. He takes the hand of Jesus and then deliberately chooses to tell the devil to get lost.

This is very much the same concept. Our words carry power! When you speak words into the earth, things happen! With every healing and miracle Jesus did, He said something. He did not nod or do a dance. He said something.

When he raised Lazarus from the dead, He said, "Come forth!" He did not just stand around praying to God. In the same way a person who has repented must say out loud, "I tell you to leave in the name of Jesus! The hold I have given to you I now take back. Get lost!"

Once they have prayed, you can step in and stand in agreement. If you flow in the gift of discerning of spirits, you might see the demon in the spirit you are dealing with and you will also be able to sense if the prayer was effective.

These are the same steps that you would follow if you are praying for inner healing or helping someone break free of the bondage that they got themselves into through a recent sin.

STEP 4: HEALING

Like I shared in the Ministry of Inner Healing chapter, very often a lot of bondage comes through the reactions of hurts in our lives. If the open door that you found relates to a situation where a hurt occurred, then you need to follow through with healing.

In cases such as witchcraft, deception or receiving contaminated impartations, then you will not need this step. However, if the open door came through abuse or any other kind of hurt, you need to ask the Holy Spirit to come and heal that hurt once and for all.

SOME SIGNS OF DEMONIC BONDAGE

Before ending off this chapter I would like to leave you with some points on what to look out for in someone that is in demonic bondage. Although you cannot use these as a "hard and fast" rule, they are some of what I have experienced in my own ministry and also what is clear in the Word.

1. CONTINUAL LYING

The Word says that satan is the father of lies. When someone has a habit of lying there is a good chance that they have a demonic bondage in their lives. Especially, when they cannot seem to control that lying.

2. UNCONTROLLABLE ANGER

Someone who lashes out and cannot seem to control themselves shows a sign of demonic bondage. Remember how I shared that the enemy takes control of the mind, emotions and will? When those emotions are completely out of their control, then something is amiss.

3. NO CONTROL OF THEIR MIND

This backs up what I shared in the previous point. This will especially manifest at times when you try to get into the Word or when the anointing begins to flow. It will seem that they suddenly do not understand anything and a "cloud of confusion" comes on them.

4. SPIRIT OF DIVINATION AND PSYCHIC ABILITIES

I think that this is pretty obvious and we sure know how Paul dealt with the "fortuneteller" that followed him around. He dealt with the demon in her and she no longer had this ability.

5. SPIRITUAL BLOCKAGES

Although this one is not a hard and fast rule, I have often found that when someone has a strong spiritual blockage that something demonic is usually the problem. This is true of someone who just cannot seem to flow in the Gifts of the Spirit or goes so far and no further in their walk with the Lord.

That blockage is often demonic in nature and I have found that when we have dealt with it, that the person breaks free miraculously and flows in all of the Gifts of the Spirit.

6. STRANGE PHYSICAL MANIFESTATIONS

I was a bit apprehensive about putting this point in, because it can be easily misunderstood. It is clear that when the Holy Spirit comes on us, that there are often physical manifestations. People will fall under the power of God. Some have been known to shake in His presence.

When Solomon dedicated the temple to God, the priests could not stand to minister. When the Early Church was spirit-filled, everyone thought they were drunk because of the way that they acted.

There are other manifestations though that are not of the Lord. This is especially true if these manifestations come when the anointing begins to flow and it interrupts the meeting - putting everyone's attention on them.

We had a couple once that had a strange manifestation. Every time the Holy Spirit came, their heads would shake violently. They had been told that this was something from the Holy Spirit. When we asked them when it started they said it started not long after they had all decided to set up a booth at a New Age fare.

After being involved there, everyone started having these manifestations. Obviously they had a backlash and by getting involved with everyone there, they picked up something that was counterfeit. What confirmed it for us as well is that they had no control of these manifestations. They prayed and renounced them. The manifestations stopped.

When you look at the manifestation ask yourself this question, "Does this line up with what I know about the Lord Jesus and His Word?"

When you know someone, you also know how they would act. You know what lines up with their nature. At the beginning of the book I shared a lot on getting to know the Lord for yourself. The more you get to know Him, the more you will know what is counterfeit.

Of course the gift of discerning of spirits is vital in helping anyone break free. Every believer should flow in this gift.

FINAL NOTE

Finally, the Lord has given you the authority in this earth to overcome any work of the enemy. Do not be afraid to stand in it. On the other hand, do not get so hung up on demons that you forget to notice that a blood bought Child of God is sitting in front of you.

The Lord has called you to mature His Bride and make Her beautiful. This part of ministry is the water that washes Her and prepares Her for the oil and perfume that will make Her lovely.

This chapter was taken from the **Minister's Handbook** written by Colette Toach.

SCRIPTURES TO MEMORIZE

Philippians 2:10 *that at the name of Jesus every knee should bow, of those in heaven, and of those on earth, and of those under the earth.*

Luke 10:19 *Behold, I give you the authority to trample on serpents and scorpions, and over all the power of the enemy, and nothing shall by any means hurt you.*

John 1:5 *And the light shineth in darkness, and the darkness comprehended it not. (KJV)*

KEY PRINCIPLES

- ✓ Demons are not walking around just "jumping" into people. If someone is demonized, then they gave that demon license.
- ✓ Talk to the person and not the demon when you minister to a believer.
- ✓ To set someone free, these are the steps to follow: Identify the open door, repentance, deliverance, healing
- ✓ The Lord has given you the authority in this earth to overcome any work of the enemy. Do not be afraid to stand in it.

PRACTICAL APPLICATION:

MULTIPLE CHOICE QUESTIONS

1. **Which one of these is NOT a step in dealing with a demon manifestation:**

   a. Know your authority
   b. Talk to the person
   c. Bring true deliverance
   d. Talk to the demon
   e. None of the above

2. **True or false?**

   You can only cast demons out of unbelievers.

3. **Which one of these is NOT a sign of bondage in the life of a believer?**

   a. Continual lying
   b. Uncontrollable anger
   c. No control of their mind
   d. Spirit of divination and psychic ability
   e. None of the above

4. **What must you do first before you can tell the devil to flee?**

   a. You must live holy
   b. You must pray and fast
   c. You must know who you are in Christ
   d. You must submit yourself to the Lord
   e. All of the above

5. **Complete this sentence: Demons do not just go around jumping into people. They have been given license through _____.**

   a. Contamination from watching horror movies
   b. Associating with the unsaved
   c. Other believers
   d. Sin
   e. All of the Above

6. **True or false?**

   Only mature believers have the authority to trample on serpents and scorpions and all the power of the enemy.

Answers: 1. d, 2. True, 3. e, 4. e, 5. d, 6. False

EXTRA NOTES

CHAPTER 05

NIGHTMARES, DECEPTION AND DEMONIC DREAMS

Chapter 05 – Nightmares, Deception and Demonic Dreams

Chapter Reference: *The Way of Dreams and Visions*, Chapter 9

IDENTIFYING DECEPTION

In this chapter we will be looking at the 'not too nice' side of dream and vision interpretation. My hope it that this will not discourage you, but rather encourage you to look for the Word of the Lord in your life, and to avoid those words and negative impressions that are not of the Spirit of God. This will promote you to maturity, to strength, and to faith, hope and love in the Lord.

I would like to begin with Job 4:15-19

> *"Then a spirit passed before my face; the hair on my body stood up.*
>
> *It stood still, but I could not discern its appearance. A form was before my eyes; There was silence; Then I heard a voice saying:*
>
> *'Can a mortal be more righteous than God? Can a man be more pure than his Maker?*
>
> *If He puts no trust in His servants, If He charges His angels with error,*
>
> *How much more those who dwell in houses of clay, whose foundation is in the dust, who are crushed before a moth?"*

I have chosen this passage as our key passage because it displays very clearly all elements of deception. It displays fear, it displays condemnation, and it questions the Word of God. All of these are very clear signs of deception.

3 CATEGORIES OF DECEPTIVE DREAMS

I will begin by breaking down deception into three main categories. Those will be: Dreams that you have where the events actually occur; those dreams and visions you receive where that revelation is false; and finally when the Lord truly does give a Word, but then the revelation is misinterpreted. Once again, as I covered in the first chapter, even though dreams are something that you have when you are asleep, they are very much like any other gift of the Spirit. They are simply night visions.

What I will share in this chapter does not only apply to dream interpretation, but it applies to any revelation that you receive from the Lord. As you start out, the possibilities are stronger that the Lord will begin speaking to you in dark sayings in your dreams. So as you begin to apply these principles in those dark sayings, and then move into a clearer understanding of His voice in visions and direct words of knowledge, wisdom and prophecy, you can continue to apply these principles to your strengthening, maturing and growing in the Lord.

1ST CATEGORY: EVENTS THAT ACTUALLY OCCUR

The first category of deception occurs where a person dreams of horrific events that actually happen. These usually fall into the external type of category where you watch an event from the outside, and it looks very much like an external prophetic dream pertaining to somebody else. A typical situation would be of you dreaming of someone's death; dreaming they are having a heart attack or stroke; dreaming that a child dies. These all fall into this category.

I found a good passage in Jeremiah 29:8-9 which says:

> *"For thus says the Lord of hosts, the God of Israel: Do not let your prophets and your diviners who are in your midst deceive you, nor listen to your dreams which you cause to be dreamed.*
>
> *For they prophesy falsely to you in My name; I have not sent them, says the Lord."*

I have had a lot of experiences where prophets in particular have written to me with dreams that they have had about actual occurrences. One such incident was when a dream was submitted about a certain child that had been mutilated in a car accident. The lady who had the 'dream' woke in a state after dreaming of a boy being hit by a truck and the remains that were left. She woke and even continued to see the events in vision. She looked out her window and 'saw' this child mutilated and could still hear his cries in her ears. She described him right down to the clothing he was wearing. The part that concerned me was that the very next day she was called to the hospital, as her sister's son had been involved in a serious accident. When she went to see the child, he was wearing the same clothing she saw in her dream. The child died.

Well, I do not think you even need the gift of discerning of spirits for the hair to stand up on your head, to know that this is not of the Lord.

DIVINATION

Such dreams and revelation in the Scripture are commonly known as "divination." If you look up the word divination in the Hebrew you will find the words related to it are "soothsaying" and "foretelling," neither of which are from the Spirit of God. God does not foretell by soothsaying. He declares His will to His prophets and to His people, so that they might speak forth His Word into the earth and bring His will to manifest in the natural. The Lord is not in the business of fortune telling for your common interest and knowledge. He is not in the business of foretelling for self-promotion and financial gain. That is not how the Lord works. Unfortunately, this is something that has become very prevalent today as people are starting to move into the gifts of the Spirit.

We have received many applications since we launched the Prophetic School, where an applicant will say very clearly, "I am a prophet, because I dream of things before they happen. I have received this gift from God, because even before I was saved, I received revelation about people and personal information. I know what's going to happen to them before it does. I dreamt of when my brother died, my auntie died, my best friend died. I dreamt of this before they died."

This revelation is NOT from the Spirit of God. And if you are experiencing this type of revelation, I want you to know right now that this is a spirit of divination. It is a spirit of witchcraft. It is of Satan, and you have given the enemy a hold in your life somewhere, that he has been able to step in and deceive you, coming in the guise of the revelation of the Lord.

The Lord is not in the business of promoting death, or promoting fear and doubt and condemnation. And these are all elements that divination promotes. You need to be very clear on this, particularly if you are using this training method to interpret the dreams of others. When somebody comes to you saying, "These dreams actually happened," particularly if they are negative, or if they are speaking of death and circumstances that have occurred that are negative, you need to be very wary, because this is not how the Lord works. He does not work in divination and soothsaying and foretelling. He works to the building up of the saints, in faith and in hope and in love, bringing His people to a place of maturity and relationship with Him.

A good example of divination in the Word is in Acts 16:16 where you find Paul being followed around by a woman with the spirit of divination, in which she was declaring, *"These men are the servants of the Most High God, who proclaim to us the way of salvation."* It sounded like she was telling the truth, didn't it? I was always frustrated when I read that Scripture because I said, "How could this woman have been a false prophet when she was speaking the actual truth? They were servants of the Most High God. Is that not what she was saying?"

But if you read between the lines she was saying, they are proclaiming a way to the Kingdom of Heaven. So in amongst that truth was a word that was shifting the people's emphasis away from one true God. And you know the story of how Paul turned around and told that spirit of divination to come out of her in the name of Jesus. And he caused a mighty ruckus in that city because of it and ended up being arrested.

But you see how the deception is, in that Satan comes as an angel of light. It looks so much like a revelation from the Lord. It looks so much like it could be truth. In fact, did it not happen that if you had a dream that somebody died and it did happen, isn't it obviously of the Lord? Just like this woman was saying, "They are servants of the Most High God," was she not speaking the truth?

Satan comes as an angel of light and you need to get into a relationship with the Lord Jesus where you can discern what is of light and what is of darkness. Only one called to the Prophetic Ministry can stand in the Office of Prophet and declare forth the Word of the Lord for the future. And only a mature prophet is called to stand up and speak this Word for the future. The Lord will not reveal it to you if you are not standing in that Office. If you have not even moved into the Prophetic Ministry and you are having these strange and horrific dreams of things really happening, I would sit up and take notice, because it is not from the Spirit of God.

2ND CATEGORY: FALSE REVELATION

The next from of deception comes as false revelation. This is slightly different from divination in that the revelation is obviously false. It is simply a lie, a deception, an accusation put in the mind of the receiver that does not come to pass and is truly a false revelation. It is entirely possible to have a dream in which the interpretation is totally out of order.

A very good example of this is Zechariah 10:2

> "For the idols speak delusion; the diviners envision lies, and tell false dreams; they comfort in vain. Therefore, the people wend their way like sheep; they are in trouble because there is no shepherd."

False interpretation scatters the flock. It brings confusion, it brings doubt and it brings discouragement in the heart of the receiver. It does not leave them with a direct path to follow. They are put on the wrong track. When coming to the Lord to receive revelation from a dream or vision that you have a received, as a very clear guideline, look at yourself first. See first if the revelation applies to you, before you stand up and start proclaiming that it is for everybody else. You are still on safe ground when you are looking at yourself and saying, "Does this apply to me?" But when you start speaking it forth and it is not of God, you will find yourself in a situation where the word you spoke does not come to pass. It is a deception and you will be leading people astray.

People think that because the Lord has given them a gift to speak forth His revelation, they can just stand up and declare it without stopping for a moment to see if it lines up with the Word of God and the Spirit of God, before speaking it forth. Always line up everything you receive from your spirit with both the Word of the Lord and the Spirit of the Lord, because the Lord Jesus will not contradict Himself. As we go on I will give you some very clear signs to watch out for in your dreams, that will indicate whether the revelation is false or deceptive.

3RD CATEGORY: MISINTERPRETING REVELATION

The third form of deception lies in the misinterpretation of dreams and visions. Misinterpretation is when the Lord will give you a revelation that is indeed a pure revelation from the Holy Spirit, but that revelation is then interpreted incorrectly. Perhaps the Lord has indeed spoken and moved on you, perhaps by giving you a symbol, a picture, a circumstance to meditate on that is a true revelation. But what happens is that the person in question takes that revelation and twists it to suit the understanding and logic of their own human mind. When you start messing around with the revelation that the Lord has given you, and start applying your own logic and your own common understanding and knowledge of the world, you are starting to get into trouble.

The greatest mistake I have seen in this area is when a person receives a dream that is clearly internal and they interpret it externally. Because when they look at the interpretation of the dream they think, "Well, this couldn't possibly be for me. The Lord couldn't possibly be saying I am out of order. This word must be for the Church." So they stand up and proclaim this magnificent dream that is clearly relating to them, and they relate it to the body of Christ, or to their congregation, and then they use it as a whip of revelation.

You need to be very discerning. When you are the star character of the dream, it is internal. Do not take an internal dream and interpret it externally to meet the desires of your own heart and your own flesh and to say, "Thus saith the Lord…" especially when you are moving in revelation for the first time and you have only just begun to receive revelation from your own spirit. This is a very clear guideline to follow.

I remember one incident where a dream was submitted to us for interpretation and the person in question had included their external 'magnificent' interpretation. Now, this person was particularly against the revival movement. She was not exactly in agreement with the manifestations and concentration and the hype on the revival movement that was sweeping across the nations.

So she took this dream, which was very clearly internal, of an incident where she came to a bar and there was a person sitting there reading the Word. The clear internal interpretation was the Spirit of God saying to her, "You need to go and receive of My joy and My Spirit." It had a very positive connotation. The Lord was saying, "You need to get into this revival anointing. You need to get in there where My Spirit is flowing, so that you can taste of it and see that it is good and have joy in your heart, and move into the next stage of your ministry."

But because she had the preconceived ideas in her mind of what she stood against, she interpreted it to mean that the church was running after this as if it was a worldly thing; as if it was something that was sinful and looking after the lusts of the flesh. She interpreted it totally externally and so used it as a whip against the revival movement, which she stood against.

Do not take the revelations the Lord has given you and add your own dogmatic ideas and preconceived ideas to it without first measuring it up with the Word of God along with the witness of the Holy Spirit. Remain teachable. Keep your heart open, and allow the Holy Spirit to change you. For as long as you keep your heart open to Him in contriteness and humility, He will not stop from pouring His Spirit into you and encouraging you, and leading you in the direction that He wants you to go.

It says in Jeremiah 23:36

"And the oracle of the Lord you shall mention no more. For every man's word will be his oracle, for you have perverted the words of the living God, the Lord of hosts, our God."

Do not take the words that the Lord has given you and pervert them with your own words and your own dogmatic ideas and doctrines.

This chapter was taken from the book **The Way of Dreams and Visions** written by Colette Toach.

SCRIPTURES TO MEMORIZE

Jeremiah 29:8-9 *For thus says the Lord of hosts, the God of Israel: Do not let your prophets and your diviners who are in your midst deceive you, nor listen to your dreams which you cause to be dreamed.*

For they prophesy falsely to you in My name; I have not sent them, says the Lord.

KEY PRINCIPLES

The 3 categories of deceptive dreams:

- ✓ Events that actually occur
- ✓ False revelation
- ✓ Misinterpretation

PRACTICAL APPLICATION:

1. **GIVE AN EXAMPLE OF ANY REVELATION THAT YOU HAVE COME ACROSS THAT WAS CLEARLY A SPIRIT OF DIVINATION.**

    You might not have experienced this for yourself, but perhaps you can identify it in someone else's actions.

    _____

    _____

    _____

    _____

    _____

2. **SHARE A CLEAR DECEPTION YOU RECEIVED YOURSELF.**

    You might not have experienced this yet. If you have, then share honestly. However, if you have not experienced this, you can put it aside for later on in your training.

    _____
    _____
    _____
    _____
    _____
    _____
    _____

3. **SHARE A REVELATION WHERE YOU MISINTERPRETED THE VISION TO FIT YOUR OWN IDEAS.**

    This is one of the first mistakes all budding prophets make. There is nothing wrong with making mistakes, as long as you are willing to learn from them.

    _____
    _____
    _____
    _____
    _____
    _____

4. WHAT DOES FALSE REVELATION BRING TO A CHURCH WHEN IT IS SHARED?

_____

_____

_____

_____

EXTRA NOTES

_____

_____

_____

_____

_____

_____

_____

_____

_____

_____

_____

Chapter 06

Satanic Attack in Dreams

Chapter 06 – Satanic Attack in Dreams

Chapter Reference: *The Way of Dreams and Visions*, Chapter 11

I want to go on now, and discuss in particular how Satan attacks in our dreams. These dreams do not have any interpretation whatsoever. They are clearly an attack from the enemy in your sleep. They are pure nightmares in which demons appear in your dreams; in which you are fighting demons and demons are fighting you, or you are dying or drowning or something to that effect. Those are the kind of dreams where wake up and the hair is standing up on the back of your neck and you feel that presence in your room; that familiar presence of fear. And you know that Satan has attacked you in your sleep.

I cover in the *Prophetic Warrior Book* and *the Stain of Sin - Overcoming Curses* message, how to overcome the enemy in his attacks. I would recommend that you go and listen to, or read these materials. It is a foundational principle of everything that we share in our teachings. Satan actually has no right whatsoever over you, because of the Blood of Christ. He has no hold on you. Satan cannot just walk up to you at any time he pleases and pick on you. It is not the way it works. If Satan had the license to do that, he would have wiped out every believer by now. But he cannot, because he comes across the Blood, and he starts to cringe.

However, if Satan attacks you then he has license to attack you. If the enemy is attacking you in your sleep then there is an open door in your life and you are saying, "Here devil please come in. Would you a like a seat? Tea, coffee, juice?" He has gained entry. And if he has attacked you directly like that in your sleep, you are not a victim, you invited him. You need to determine how you invited him, and that is why I would like to encourage you to go and listen to or read that chapter, because it is too extensive for me to cover in detail here. I will however just touch on some of the points.

CONTAMINATED OBJECTS

Perhaps it could be that you have brought something, an object perhaps, into your home that has been contaminated. Just like Achan in the days of Joshua, when they went and defeated Jericho and he brought those objects into the tents of Israel. What happened is that Israel was suddenly defeated by their enemies. They cried out and said, "Lord, why?" And the Lord showed them that they had brought cursed objects into their camp, and it caused Satan to defeat them. Even so, you may have brought an object into your home, and it may have caused you to open the door to the enemy.

One example of this is of a couple who came to me, and their child was continually having nightmares. They had prayed with her, they had stood with her, and nothing they did stopped these nightmares, until they asked somebody to come and pray with them. And they saw, above the bed, a wall hanging. The minister kept being drawn to this wall hanging.

He said, "Where did you receive that from?"

It turned out that a foreign couple had given it to the child as a gift. If I am not mistaken I believe it was a Chinese wall hanging. But the point was, it was contaminated. It had been prayed over Satanically, and they had now brought this object into the child's room and placed it above her bed and this poor child could not sleep. She was having nightmares continuously. Obviously she was having nightmares continuously! They had invited Satan right into her bedroom and hung him over her bed! They simply prayed over the hanging and dedicated it to the Lord, and the nightmares stopped.

I have even had occasions with my own children, where I have brought things into their room, gifts sometimes that people have given, even sometimes magazines that have not had the Spirit of the Lord on them. I put it in their room and they have a spirit of restlessness in them and they come to us in the middle of the night with nightmares. When I go to investigate where Satan has gotten a hold, most of the time something has been put in their room that has been contaminated; an object.

THROUGH PEOPLE

Contamination and license can also come from your association with people that are not walking in the blessing of the Lord. They carry a curse within them. Perhaps they have been involved in the occult. Perhaps they are just believers that have gotten involved in things that they should not be getting involved in, and they carry on them that spirit of deception and divination. As you make contact with this person, your spirits connect, you pick up a contamination, and you carry it home with you. You open the door and let Satan right in. That night as you are going to sleep you are attacked time and time again.

I know, I have had this happen to me on many occasions, where I come across false prophets and come into confrontation with them, and I have very irresponsibly, forgotten to break the links with them. That night I cannot sleep for the nightmares that are assailing me. The minute I close my eyes, Satan uses that opportunity to attack me in my sleep. Such a coward, the enemy is. All I do is I wake up, break the links, and I tell Satan to get. It is really that simple.

The curses could be passed down from generations or from associations. Like I said, I am not going to cover it in detail. But if you are being attacked by demons in your sleep on a continual basis, Satan has an inroad. He has been given license. I would recommend you look around your room, see what you have brought into the room or into your home, and ask the Spirit of the Lord to open your eyes to where Satan has gained this hold on your life.

PRACTICALITIES

In conclusion, I would like you to take the dreams that you have written out, and I am going to go through that dream with you bit by bit now and show you how to identify whether it is a deception or not. Then I am going to show you how to identify, yet again, if it internal, healing, purging or garbage. This is the practical part of the chapter, so you can pull out your Workbook, pen and paper, and you can begin agreeing or disagreeing with the points that I am covering...

DECEPTIVE DREAMS

The very first thing... I want you to discard this dream as not of the Lord, if it has any of the following points:

- ✓ Firstly, discard the dream if you wake up with that spirit of fear attacking you, where you feel like the room is closing in on you, where you feel paralyzed. This dream was not of God.

- ✓ If you feel condemned, if you are not immediately moved to conviction and weep before the Lord and give Him this matter, but are feeling pushed once again into paralysis and depression, this was not the Spirit of God. Disregard this revelation.

- ✓ If you wake feeling accused, where lies are coming up in your head over and over again like, "Did you know you did this? And then you did that? And then you did this? Then you lied to this person and you treated this person like that. You did this sin, and you did that sin." That is not from the Lord. The Spirit of God brings conviction, in which you repent and are motivated to action. You are not discouraged to paralysis.

- ✓ If you feel compelled strongly to act on the dream immediately, this dream is not of the Lord, because the Spirit of God does not push. You feel like you are pushed from behind, from outside, like there is a pressure upon you to perhaps conform, to "do." Where something says in your dream, "Rise up and do it now.

Act now, now, now!" This is not the Lord and I would submit this revelation to somebody who has a bit more experience in dream interpretation to sense the spirit on it if you are not quite able to do so yourself.

Now, you have identified whether the dream was a deception or not. If it is a deception, tear it up, throw it away and tell Satan to take his lies and get out. If you have opened a door to the enemy close it, but do not entertain the thoughts of that revelation any longer. Do not allow it to sow its seed of doubt, fear and condemnation.

The following is an example of such a dream. I would like you to note the points I just mentioned above in this dream:

DREAM: LADY IN BLACK

"In this dream there was a woman dressed in black from head to foot, including wearing a black veil over her face. Every time I watched myself talking to my husband he could not seem to hear me. However, whenever this woman in black spoke to him she would only whisper in his ears and he would respond by pointing his finger at me.

The next thing I was inside the dream, in a courtroom standing beside my husband and facing a judge. The same woman in black was standing on the other side of him. The judge told me that they had come to an arrangement about our three sons and that they were going to my husband. My husband only spoke up when this woman in black whispered in his ears. Again, the judge did not seem to hear me when I spoke. This is what the judge said to me. "You can see your children every four days and every fourth weekend." I remembered crying and crying. We walked out of the courtroom while this woman in black continued to walk on the other side of my husband.

Suddenly, I was outside of the dream watching myself. I was in our living room sitting on the settee opposite my mother who was asking me how it happened that my husband got the children. My mother then repeated the very same sentence the judge had spoken to me earlier "four days and every fourth month". Then in the dream I watched myself take two glasses and a bottle of wine. I placed the bottle on the floor near my feet. Just as I did this my husband burst into the room with the same woman in black at his side. He shouted at me, "Yes that is it! You are an alcoholic. That's right, that is what you are." I woke up.

In reality I am not an alcoholic, nor have I ever been. It is a known truth that I adore my children with a passion. Our marriage is good and we are not at all divided."

(**NOTE:** Your first reaction would be to look up the symbols and try to interpret this dream. It looks so like a straightforward internal dream, but if you would apply the principles I stated, you will see the deception in it. To try and interpret such a dream would lead you further into deception. Also note that the negative emphasis in this dream does not line up with the real relationship she has with her husband.)

MY INTERPRETATION:

"Upon reading your dream, something did not sit right on my spirit. Upon further study of your dream I noted something that I would like you to see. (Please note the principles here that I have written on deception. I would like you to see for yourself, what I have sensed here.)

I sensed all of these elements in your dream. There was fear, there was a lot of accusation and I also sensed that 'forcefulness'. This dream is a false revelation from the enemy and I would like to suggest that you close the door to any inroad you may have given Satan. There is no interpretation as it is a clear deception, so please reject it entirely."

Her response confirmed what I sensed.

RESPONSE:

God bless you and thank you Colette for such a speedy response. I actually woke up feeling the following:

Paralyzed into not pressing on with the things of the God.

Condemnation did set in and doubts about unworthiness and it was easier to for me to be quiet. If my voice was heard, then I will be discredited and shamed.

Yes, I did feel the pressure to conform to a superficial relationship with the Lord.

EMOTIONS

Now that you have read your dream through and are sure it is not a deception, the first thing I want you to jot down is the emotion of the dream. How did you feel? Did you feel victorious? Did you feel fearful? Did you feel jealous? Did you feel strong? Did you feel insecure? Once you have determined the emotion of the dream, it actually gives you a very good path to run on, because now you know the emphasis. You know whether the emphasis is going to be one of needing healing, or an emphasis of one where you are already victorious and moving into something wonderful that the Lord has for you.

Look at the emotion of your dream. Was it healing? Did you wake up having faced a situation that you were victorious over? Not all negative emotions denote a negative dream, so do not see jealousy and anger as specifically negative dreams. It could be that you are a very quiet person, and in your dream you rise up in anger and act against a situation. This could very well be the Spirit of the Lord encouraging you to stand up and express yourself.

Even the Word says that God is a jealous God. Jealousy is not a sin. It is a natural, human emotion. Anger is not a sin, for the Word says, *"Be angry, but do not sin."* Anger is meant to motivate you to positive action, as is jealousy.

So do not see the emotions of the dream as necessarily a negative influence, because the Lord might be trying to get a message across to you that says, "Perhaps you need more of this emotion in your life." Or perhaps, "You need less of this emotion in your life." Or even perhaps, "This is where I'm leading you. You need to be angrier. You need to be angry for Me. You need to have righteous indignation. You need to be jealous over My people. I want you to be jealous over My people!"

Can you see how identifying the emotion of a dream gives you a very good track to run on? You need to determine if it is negative or positive. Your emotions will pretty much give you a track to run on. Ask yourself, "Did I wake up feeling as if something was amiss in my spirit? There is perhaps something negative in my life that needs to be dealt with."

I am not talking about condemnation. I am talking about that deep stirring inside that says, "I need to deal with this area of my life." Or, "I've gone off the path that the Lord has had me on. I need to get back on it."

If you are dreaming that you are driving along in your car and suddenly your car goes off the road, this has a negative connotation, in which it could be saying, "You were on the right track, but you're being sidetracked. You need to get back onto the path again." Or perhaps you have been dreaming that you have been driving on the side of the road and suddenly you turn off onto a main highway. This dream would have a very positive connotation in that it is saying, "You were off the track, but you are on the right track again."

Of course, I am referring here specifically to internal dreams. Identify whether it is something negative in your life that needs to be fixed, or something positive that the Lord is motivating you towards.

WHAT TYPE OF DREAM?

Now identify if your dream is healing, purging, garbage or prophetic.

HEALING DREAMS

In your dream, did you perhaps dream of past events that you were victorious over? Did you perhaps dream of characters from the past, friends from the past, teachers of the past, even buildings of the past? Were there smells that you were familiar with from the past; colors that represented something from the past? Anything that perhaps relates to childhood and adolescence, but in the dream you had victory.

Perhaps you have had a bad relationship with your mother, but in your dream, you and her are embracing and a bond is formed. This is a healing dream. This is the Lord taking away the hurt and anguish that has been in you, and He is just saying, "I'm healing this area of your life. You won't need to worry about it anymore." If that is the case, if you are dreaming about circumstances that are very familiar to you and you are having victory, it is a healing dream, in which case it has no clear interpretation other than it is just the Lord confirming His work in your life.

PURGING DREAMS

Perhaps you are dreaming that you are giving into temptation. This would be your purging dream, in which your subconscious is simply letting out in your mind all those stimuli which you have been feeding into it during the day. Perhaps you got mad at your boss and you really felt like hitting him, and in your dream you are actually beating the stuffing out of him. This would simply indicate a purging dream. It does not have an interpretation other than it was just your inner man living out your fears, temptations and ambitions in your dream.

Perhaps you are dreaming that you have won the lottery, or maybe you are dreaming that you are laying your hands on people and they are just falling under the power. This is not necessarily a prophetic dream. It could very simply be the desires of your heart. It is just a purging dream, and your subconscious is throwing out all those inner desires and conflicts and everything that you have been feeding in.

I know I have had many people submit dreams in which they are saying, "I was standing in front of this huge congregation. I went along the healing line, and every single person was healed and fell under the power."

It is a great dream and it could even be the Lord confirming the call on a person's life, but that is not necessarily a prophetic word, other than simply the desire of the person's heart. If somebody has a keen desire for evangelism they could dream that they are evangelizing the nations. That is not necessarily prophetic. It could simply be their inner desires that are being displayed in their dreams. So it is very important to get the background information of the person whose dream you are interpreting, so you can place the dream in the context where it belongs.

GARBAGE DREAMS

Garbage dreams are very clear to identify. Those are your movie dreams. Those are when you say; "If I could have put that dream into a script it would have been a billion dollar production." It is one of those dreams, where you are dreaming of aliens and space ships, and models and who knows what else. There are many different scene changes one after the other with complicated characters in them. It is a very complex dream with a lot of detail and stimuli, a lot of feelings, a lot of changes and a lot of activity.

This is very clearly a garbage dream. I have had people come to me with dreams that are six pages long and they say, "I gave this dream to you in detail. What is its interpretation? It was so clear. It must have an interpretation."

It had scene change after scene change. They went to town, then they were at home, then they were in the basement, and then they were on the roof. Then this person came to them and said this, and then another person came and said, "No, what that person's saying is not right." Then they were speaking to this person, and then... It is a garbage dream.

The Spirit of God is not a God of confusion, and if He gives you revelation, He will not mince His words and He will not contradict Himself. He will give you a very clear and simple word. A dream with many scene changes, that is overcomplicated, and that usually went through the entire evening of your sleep is just your mind throwing out the garbage that you have been feeding into it since the day you were born.

PROPHETIC DREAMS

As you know, there are three types of prophetic dreams. In this dream, were you the star character? If you can say 'yes', tick it off, it is internal. If 'no', if you were standing out on the outside looking in, it was an external prophetic dream.

Was the dream very simple? A dream that is from the Holy Spirit will be very simple. And it is entirely possible that you will have three quick dreams one after the other, all with the same message, just as in the days of Joseph where Pharaoh dreamt of the seven cows and then of the seven ears of wheat. They were two very quick dreams with the same emphasis and message. So if the Lord is really trying to get something across to you, usually prophetically, He will give you a couple of dreams or visions, one after the other, that all have the same emphasis, the same emotion and sometimes even the same numbers or colors. Perhaps something specific will stand out in the dream. In the case of Pharaoh the number seven was specific in his dream, and the lean and the fat.

So, if you have had a few quick dreams, and all of them are clear, pick out the symbols in each dream that were very prominent and write them down. The internal prophetic dream will also be very clear, but it usually pertains to your ministry or future events. It does not pertain to your current spiritual condition, as does the straight internal dream.

Perhaps in your dream you have a key and you are opening a door. The Lord could very well be saying, "I am going to be leading you into the prophetic. You will be using what I have given you on behalf of others." That could be an internal prophetic dream.

Perhaps you dream of a situation of where you are in a church, an old-style building, you are leaving and it is being burnt behind you. The Lord is saying, "I'm taking you out of that religious mindset. You are going to be moving on."

Perhaps you are dreaming of putting coffins in the ground, or of dead bodies. This could very well be an internal dream, or even a prophetic dream where the Lord is saying, "There is a part of your flesh that needs to die, and you won't let it die. Let it go!"

Next time we are going to go into characters and symbols and you will be able to pull out the pieces and begin to interpret your dreams and visions piece by piece. But firstly I want you to understand how to identify the emotion and then to identify what type of dream it is, before you begin the actual interpretation of symbols. It is no use trying to interpret a dream that has no interpretation. It is no use taking a demonic revelation and trying to interpret it by the Spirit of God. It does not work. It is no use taking a dream that is just simply your mind throwing out garbage and trying to interpret it, as you will confuse yourself and you will go on to confuse others too. And you are going to end up in hot water, because people are not going to be impressed.

EXTERNAL PROPHETIC DREAMS

In the external prophetic dream, obviously this is where you are standing out looking in. Once again, it is a very clear dream. It is not overcomplicated, but it does tend to have a bit more detail and the symbols will be very clear. You will see specific characters and symbols that will be very clear as to what they represent.

It has a future orientation. The external prophetic dream operates as the word of wisdom in that it has a future orientation. Another good way to identify if a dream is externally prophetic is that the characters that you usually use in your internal dreams cannot be interpreted. The symbols are common to you. You see, the Holy Spirit will always bring up from your spirit and mind, symbols that are common to you. As we discussed in King Nebuchadnezzar's dream, the Lord used an illustration of an idol; a big statue with its head of gold and so on. The Lord will use symbols that are very common in your internal dreams, so that you can understand His message.

You will dream of people that you are familiar with, and so from that familiarity you can identify what they symbolize. In an external dream the symbols and characters in your dream are not of the usual sort. They are perhaps people you have never met before, and they are perhaps symbols that you have never had in your dreams before. But like I said, the external dream is specifically geared towards the Prophetic Ministry. So if you have been having those kinds of dreams, it could be that the Lord is leading you into that Office.

Next time we will take a look at characters and people in your dreams; how to look at them, analyze your relationships with them, and determine what they mean in your dreams. And so you are going to discover that they are used often for a reason, because the Holy Spirit is trying to use them to get a message across to you. And it will be very exciting next time as you start looking at the practical application.

But for now, I want you to take this chapter and I want you to apply it to your life. I want you to stand against any deception that Satan might have put in you, and to put it aside. Do not dwell on it. Do not allow yourself to be discouraged. Simply deal with the open door and put it away. Then open your heart to the Spirit of the Lord and say, "Lord, I am here. Speak to me."

This chapter was taken from the book **The Way of Dreams and Visions** written by Colette Toach.

SCRIPTURE TO MEMORIZE

Isaiah 54:17 *No weapon formed against you shall prosper, and every tongue which rises against you in judgment you shall condemn. This is the heritage of the servants of the Lord, and their righteousness is from Me, Says the Lord.*

KEY PRINCIPLES

- ✓ Discard a dream if you wake up with that spirit of fear attacking you. This dream was not of the Lord.
- ✓ If you wake up condemned and accused, the dream was not of the Lord.
- ✓ If you feel compelled strongly to act on the dream immediately, this dream is not of the Lord, because the Spirit of God does not push.

PRACTICAL APPLICATION:

1. **THINK BACK ON ANY NIGHTMARES YOU MIGHT HAVE HAD IN THE PAST.**

_____

_____

_____

_____

_____

_____

_____

2. CAN YOU REMEMBER THE EVENTS IN YOUR LIFE THAT SURROUNDED THAT TIME?

_____
_____
_____
_____

3. IT IS IMPORTANT THAT YOU IDENTIFY WHERE EXACTLY THE ENEMY HAD AN OPEN DOOR TO ATTACK YOU AT THAT TIME.

_____
_____
_____
_____

4. IF YOU ARE STILL STRUGGLING WITH NIGHTMARES, THEN HE STILL HAS AN OPEN DOOR, AND YOU NEED TO TAKE A GOOD LOOK AT YOUR OWN LIFE AND RELATIONSHIPS.

5. A GOOD PLACE TO START WOULD BE TO GO THROUGH YOUR BEDROOM AND SEE IF YOU HAVE BROUGHT ANYTHING INTO IT THAT IS CONTRARY TO THE WORD AND SPIRIT OF THE LORD.

6. WRITTEN MATERIALS SUCH AS BOOKS, MAGAZINES, LETTERS OR NEWSPAPERS ARE A GOOD STARTING POINT.

7. AFTER THAT LOOK FOR ANY ORNAMENTS OR OBJECTS THAT YOU BROUGHT IN AROUND THE TIME YOUR NIGHTMARES BEGAN.

8. IF YOU STILL CANNOT FIND ANYTHING, THEN LOOK TO THE LORD TO REVEAL ANY NEW RELATIONSHIPS OR EVEN OLD FRIENDS YOU HAVE STRUCK UP A

RELATIONSHIP WITH THAT ARE UNDER A CURSE. ALSO CONSIDER THINGS YOU READ OR RECENTLY WATCHED AND OPENED YOUR HEART TO.

Above all else, ask the Lord for revelation to direct you to where the open door is. We do not want to go on a "witch hunt," but simply want to find that open door to the enemy and close it in Jesus' name!

EXTRA NOTES

CHAPTER 07

LOGIC, DECEPTION AND SPIRIT OF DIVINATION CHECKLIST

Chapter 07 – Logic, Deception, and Spirit of Divination Checklist

Chapter Reference: *The Way of Dreams and Visions Student Manual*, Lesson 8

It is not a lot of fun to admit that you have gotten into deception. By now though, you should be realizing that it is part and parcel of prophetic training. The spirit of divination and deception though are quite different and I want to help you identify the difference here.

Below are three checklists for you to help sort your revelations out. In Lesson 9, I also include a checklist for a revelation that is truly of God. For now though, I want you to learn to discern the difference between these.

LOGIC AND PRECONCEIVED IDEA CHECKLIST

Often we want an answer so badly that we come up with something! Although these revelations are not damaging, they do not have any power to help either. They are logical and are filled with your own ideas.

1. The revelation does not come as a surprise to you. It is something you already thought.

2. The revelation supports your own assessment of someone.

3. Your revelation comes with anger and frustration.
4. When your word is not received, you are angry and you feel that you need to be justified.

5. You want the word to come to pass so badly because your reputation or what you want hangs on it.

6. The revelation tells you what you want to hear.

7. Your revelation backs up the counsel you would have given that person yourself.

8. The revelation you bring is a complete surprise to the person. Not only is it something they never thought of before, but it is also nothing that the

Lord indicated before. Although revelation can often tell us things we did not know, when you hear it, it witnesses with your spirit.

DECEPTION CHECKLIST

This kind of revelation comes in two forms. The first is when the revelation is simply not from the Lord, but from the enemy. The second is when a revelation starts out as from the Lord, but the enemy takes it and pushes it beyond what God intended.

1. You feel stressed and pushed to bring the word.

2. The revelation goes directly against the Word.

3. The revelation you bring causes confusion to the person you bring it to, because it cuts directly across everything God has ever told them.

4. You feel guilty or full of fear in either bringing or not bringing the word.

5. The word puts the person into a state of fear or condemnation so that their spiritual life starts to suffer.

6. After giving that word, a clear curse starts to manifest in that person's life.

7. The word exalts the speaker instead of the Lord.

8. The revelation interrupts what the Holy Spirit was trying to do at the time.

9. The revelation distracts from the message that was trying to be brought.

10. The word sidetracks the person from the conviction that God was trying to bring.

11. The revelation breaks the flow of the anointing completely.

12. You suddenly struggle to hear the voice of the Lord.
13. The revelation comes to you suddenly out of nowhere and without praying or being in ministry.

14. The revelation is very forceful and you feel compelled to share IMMEDIATELY.

Spiritual Discernment Workshop

SPIRIT OF DIVINATION CHECKLIST

This kind of revelation is a particular kind of deception that is very damaging. The danger of this kind of deception is the demonic power it carries. Things spoken forth under this spirit actually do come to pass.

This is why people do not identify it. Because it came to pass, they naturally assume it is of God. Simply because you got a revelation that happened, does not make you a prophet! Consider the priests that performed miracles to oppose Moses. Consider also the witch who summoned up Samuel – what was said came to pass, but it was certainly not God's work!

I am also including false angelic experiences in this checklist as they are directly tied to the spirit of divination.

1. You received many revelations even before becoming born again.

2. You have an experience with an angel where it pushes you to receive from it directly. The angel's face is hidden from you.

3. You are visited by an angel that does not show its face, but surrounds you in a bright light that overwhelms you.

4. You are filled with extreme fear or foreboding by the revelation you receive.

5. The revelations are usually brutal and indicate negative events of the future. These often involve death and destruction.

6. The evil things you see in your dreams or revelations come to pass.

7. Your revelations are continually negative involving murder, sexual and personal sin and many other works of the enemy.
8. Out of body experiences.

9. Experiences in the spirit where you do not have any control over your own body or mind.

10. You keep seeing lots of colorful and bright lights. (This is common in the New Age cult)

11. You continually see angels, specifically female angels and angels with wings. (Although worship angels do have wings, the New Age cult also sees these "visions." There are no female or baby angels mentioned in scripture.)

12. Continually seeing demons in the spirit – especially accompanied with fear.

13. Live manifestations of ghosts and demons. This includes audible voices that bring fear and condemnation.

14. Continual darkness and heaviness in your revelations.

15. A complete emphasis on the work of the enemy and not the work of the Lord.

16. Continually receiving revelation of demonic symbols used by mainline cults.

NOTE: I know that this is a long list, but I have included many points, not just for your own revelations, but so that you can also assess the revelations of others. If you feel that your revelations fall into any of these lists, do not be discouraged, because there is hope!

If your revelations fall into the "pre-conceived ideas" category, then do not get upset, because you have a way to go still! At the beginning it is common for a prophet in training to make mistakes. However, as the Holy Spirit begins to refine you, you will learn to die to those ideas.

That is what prophetic training is all about. Simply give up your revelations to the Lord and ask for His help.

If you suspect though that you have fallen into deception or that you might have a spirit of divination, then you need someone to stand in agreement with you.

It is not easy to deal with something like that by yourself. It is much better if you get someone to stand in agreement with you.

This chapter was taken from ***The Way of Dreams and Visions Student Manual*** written by Colette Toach.

Spiritual Discernment Workshop

EXTRA NOTES

Chapter 08

The Prophetic Super Spy

Chapter 08 – The Prophetic Super Spy

Chapter Reference: *Prophetic Counter Insurgence*, Chapter 2

There is no greater COIN warfare than sneaking behind enemy lines and setting the captives free. As a prophet, you are God's "secret spy" finding the cracks in satan's walls and finding a way to reach those he has bound.

As you rise up in your prophetic authority, you will find yourself surrounded by so many who have been bound their entire lives by the work of the enemy. You will see believers crippled by spirits of infirmity.

You will look over a wasteland that once shone as a solid marriage – now lying crumbled in ruins through an attack of strife and vainglory. You will wander into the darkest places and find King's kids feeding on the slime of lust and love of money.

Contaminated with bitterness and bound by power demons, you will be led to believers who have offered up their walk of salvation to eat with pigs. Prophet of God, you are beginning to see your calling take place in front of your eyes.

I have taught you to flow in the gifts of the Spirit. You have learned how to hear God in many ways. You have been armed to do spiritual warfare of every level. You are trained, clothed in armor and your heart has been tried in the fire.

You are ready. Soon you will learn what it means to carry the prophetic key of authority and unlock doors on behalf of the Church. For now, though, I want to lead you by the hand through an essential function of the prophet.

What is the purpose of all this anointing and authority if you do not use it for others? So you have proved that God speaks to you. So what? So you have overcome the flesh. So what?

What about the sick, broken and bruised half dying all around you? You have engaged in spiritual warfare on the battlefield. Now, let me show you what it means to truly engage in COIN warfare.

It's time to get to the nitty-gritty and get into people's lives. You will find them in satan's dungeons chained to prison walls, guarded by ruler demons. Men and women of God demonized and without hope of the future.

Remember what I shared regarding Lucifer's desire to split the Church? Using the systems of the world is just one of his tactics. The other is to get believers to invite him. You will not believe how many believers are demonized in the Church today.

Perhaps I was naïve – but I did not expect demon manifestations from those I was training. Well that naiveté sure left quickly when I experienced one manifestation after another as God moved in our meetings.

DEMONIC BONDAGE

In ministry, you are going to find so many of God's people bound by the enemy. Some will be bound in cycles of sin, or fear, that cripples them. Others will be in an even worse state and will be bound by possessing demons. In the chapters that follow I am going to teach you how to handle both kinds of oppression.

DEMONIC OPPRESSION VS. DEMONIC POSSESSION

Doing warfare in the heavenly realm opens doors in the natural realm. It will prepare the hearts of God's people and arrange circumstances for the Kingdom spies to make their way into the enemy's camp.

Often, you as the prophet, will be one of those spies. You will be the one sneaking in and removing satan's bondage from the elect. Now even in the world, when a force goes in to rescue a prisoner of war, they have to be prepared for anything.

It is not uncommon that if someone that has been in bondage for a long time, they are so used to being turned towards the cause of the enemy, that instead of being happy at being set free, they will turn on their own.

In the same way, it is essential that you understand the difference between demonic oppression and possession, because you will need to treat each one differently. Some rules remain the same for both though.

In both cases, the blood of Jesus is the solution. In both cases, repentance removes the license that satan has been given in their lives.

However, things differ greatly when it comes to the manifestation of that oppression. The difference also lies on how the person came under that bondage in the first place. Once you understand the difference, you will also know where to begin in helping to smash the chains that have them bound.

DEMONIC OPPRESSION

> *Acts 10:38 How God anointed Jesus of Nazareth with the Holy Spirit and with power, who went about doing good and healing all who were oppressed by the devil, for God was with Him.*

Strong's Concordance for the Word Oppressed:

Spiritual Discernment Workshop

2616 - katadunasteuo {kat-ad-oo-nas-tyoo'-o}

>AV - oppress 2; 2
>
>1) to exercise harsh control over one, to use one's power against one
>2) to oppress one

Simply put, demonic oppression is the result of the enemy being the bully that he is! Remember how you learned in the *Prophetic Warrior* that the enemy has 3 battlefields?

He attacks in the battlefield of the soul, the circumstances and the systems of this world. A soldier can only fight the good fight for so long, before their knees get weak. Even Samson, after killing all the Philistines with the jawbone of a donkey, was terribly weak after the event.

When you have been facing one attack after the other from the enemy, your arm gets weak. If you do not have a team, or others to help pick you up, you will find yourself faltering. Sooner or later you will become discouraged.

You will begin to believe the stones of accusation being thrown at your window. Eventually, one of those stones will break through. The continual attack on your circumstances will start to erode your faith and hope.

Before you know it, you have allowed satan license and have given into his attacks. You have allowed fear to grip you. You entertain the voices of accusation. You steal a moment to taste the gall of bitterness. You, child of God, are now in the throes of oppression.

> **KEY PRINCIPLE**
>
> Simply put – demonic oppression is the continual attack of the enemy that you eventually submit to.

That is what Acts 10:38 is talking about. In the Strong's Concordance, the word "oppression" means to exercise harsh control over. The enemy will keep attacking you until he has gained the upper hand. A wrestling match, where he eventually overcomes you.

From there, your mind is all over the place and you find it hard to take God at His Word.

> Luke 11:34 *The lamp of the body is the eye. Therefore, when your eye is good, your whole body also is full of light. But when your eye is bad, your body also is full of darkness.*
> 35 *Therefore take heed that the light which is in you is not darkness.*

What was light is now darkness. Your eye no longer sees the truth. Fear has eaten up your faith, bitterness, your love, and self-pity has consumed your hope. The light is snuffed out and it feels that the only light you have left, is darkness.

This is what oppression looks like and it is the easiest to help someone overcome.

SINS OF THE HEART

Sins of the heart are what allows satan this kind of control in our lives. The kind of control that manipulates your mind, emotions, and will. This kind of oppression confuses the mind, spikes wrong emotions, and leads to sinful and willful actions.

Someone under demonic oppression will not manifest in the same way as someone that is possessed. Instead their minds will be bound. They will struggle with things like a spirit of anger, and continual fear.

Power demons arrayed against them on every side, making so much noise that they cannot hear the Lord. In this moment, they will allow their flesh to dominate their decisions instead of their spirit.

The *Prophetic Warrior* book is all about demonic oppression and how you encounter it as a prophet. So I am not going to labor it here.

The point is, once you understand this difference, you will be ready for the next chapter, where I will teach you how to help someone in this spiritual condition.

DEMONIC POSSESSION

> Acts 16:16 *Now it happened, as we went to prayer, that a certain slave girl possessed with a spirit of divination met us, who brought her masters much profit by fortune.*

Strong's Concordance for the Word Possessed:

2192 - echo {ekh'-o}

> AV - have 613, be 22, need + 5532 12, misc 63, vr have 2; 712

1a) to have (hold) in the hand, in the sense of wearing, to have (hold) possession of the mind (refers to alarm, agitating emotions, etc.), to hold fast keep, to have or comprise or involve, to regard or consider or hold as

2) to have i.e. own, possess

2b) used of those joined to any one by the bonds of natural blood or marriage or friendship or duty or law etc., of attendance or companionship

4) to hold one's self to a thing, to lay hold of a thing, to adhere or cling to

4a) to be closely joined to a person or a thing

There is a word that keeps cropping up when you look at the Strong's Concordance translation of the word "possession," can you spot it?

You will see that in more than one place, possession is referred to as ownership. There is a drastic difference between being oppressed by the devil, and being possessed by the devil. Unfortunately, it is all lumped together and then you wonder why people do not break free!

> ### KEY PRINCIPLE
>
> The most outstanding difference between oppression and possession is that oppression comes from submitting to the continual attack of the enemy. Possession results from giving satan ownership of your body.

How do you give satan ownership? I knew you were going to ask that. It is a lot simpler than you might imagine, and when you see it for yourself, many things are going to fall into place. The secret lies in this passage,

> *1 Corinthians 6:16 Or do you not know that he who is joined to a harlot is one body with her? For the two, He says, shall become one flesh.*
> *17 But he who is joined to the Lord is one spirit with Him.*
> *18 Flee sexual immorality. Every sin that a man does is outside the body, but he who commits sexual immorality sins against his own body.*

The Word tells us that we are to present our bodies as a living sacrifice to the Lord. When we do this, we give the Holy Spirit license in our lives. In essence... He takes possession of who we are, and we become His temple.

Now, think about this for a moment. What if you yielded your body as a living sacrifice to satan? You can see where I am going with this...

> **KEY PRINCIPLE**
>
> Demonic possession is the result of yielding your body up to the service and worship of satan.

I love what it says in 1 Corinthians 6. When you give your body up to a prostitute, you are making yourself one with her! This is why the Word speaks so much about fleeing prostitution.

It is not just a case of being sinful – but the fact that when you deliberately yield up your body to satan, you give him ownership of it.

Think about it. When you engage in bitterness, you give satan license in your soul. He uses this license to manipulate your thoughts and emotions.

When you give satan license in your body through sins of the flesh, you give him license to possess and manipulate it. So when you are in praise and worship and someone manifests a demon and starts crawling around on the floor as a snake... you are seeing someone who gave license to satan through a sin of the flesh.

If you are praying with someone and they are so bound by fear that they cannot hear the Lord any longer, you are ministering to someone that is oppressed through sins of the heart. As you make this distinction, you just strapped a new sword to your side.

You will come to learn as a prophet that you will not always use the same kind of weapon. Sometimes you will use a sword, and other times, a dagger. Know which weapon to use for what.

So what kind of sins of the flesh are we talking about here? Does this mean that if I swear at my boss behind her back that I am going to wake up tomorrow morning possessed by Lucifer himself?

Relax. It takes a bit more than that! In fact, the Word lays it out so clearly for us and when I point out exactly what sins of the flesh lead to possession, it will become clear.

On a side note, are you already beginning to see why possessing demons can't just jump from one person to another? If you cast a demon out of someone who was just hissing on the floor, that demon cannot just hop, skip and jump to the next passerby and go on his merry way.

No, there are clear rules to follow. The spiritual realm has its own structure and even the enemy cannot just take what has not been given to him. So let's see exactly what gives him ownership and from there... learn how to take it away!

SINS OF THE FLESH

> *Galatians 5:19 Now the works of the flesh are evident, which are: adultery, fornication, uncleanness, lewdness,*
> *20 idolatry, sorcery, hatred, contentions, jealousies, outbursts of wrath, selfish ambitions, dissensions, heresies,*
> *21 envy, murders, drunkenness, revelries, and the like; of which I tell you beforehand, just as I also told you in time past, that those who practice such things will not inherit the kingdom of God.*

I told you the Word makes it clear! Want to see what sins of the flesh lead to possession? Take a look at the works of the flesh and you will begin to see the core of how man gives his body up to satan as a living sacrifice.

You see, that is the point of each of these sins – they are not just incorrect choices. These sins are not just mistakes or misunderstandings. Each of these sins deliberately yields the body into satan's service.

When you got saved, you submitted your spirit, soul, and body to the Lord. You made him your master. Now when man submits his body to satan, he makes satan his master.

Let us not even talk of the confusion a Christian faces when he has not fully taken away the ownership he gave satan!

I have taken the passage above and broken it down into five sins of the flesh that give satan ownership of your body, and so lead to demonic possession. I am taking advantage of the fact that at this stage of your training, you are secure enough in yourself to go through each of these points and to apply the ones to your life that are valid to your situation.

Although I used the personal pronoun "you" throughout the remaining chapter, I am not personally accusing you of sleeping with prostitutes or of beating up your spouse. Seriously... I have had people get mad at me, because they read a book and complained that I accused them of things that did not apply. (Yeah, I also shook my head in disbelief.)

However, on the rare chance that you are a "touchy feely" type and easily offended allow me to provide a disclaimer. I bring up some sensitive subjects below and just because I use the word "you" does not mean it all applies to your life.

Allow the anointing to penetrate your heart. Allow the principles to sink into your spirit. If something I say hits you like a spear in the side and you flinch... well then prophet, I have but one question to ask you, "What on earth are you doing off the cross?!"

IDOLATRY

> *1 Corinthians 10:14 Therefore, my beloved, flee from idolatry.*
>
> *1 Corinthians 10:20 Rather, that the things which the Gentiles sacrifice they sacrifice to demons and not to God, and I do not want you to have fellowship with demons.*
> *21 You cannot drink the cup of the Lord and the cup of demons; you cannot partake of the Lord's table and of the table of demons.*

This is by far the most common way that someone becomes possessed by a demon. If someone worships satan, he will take ownership. It stands to reason – you signed a contract with him that read, "I give my life over to you."

When you get born again, you give ownership to the Lord, but it is essential in this time to make it clear to satan that you are changing sides! This is what Paul meant when he spoke about having two masters.

You cannot give both God and satan ownership of your body! Sure, when you get born again, you have submitted your spirit to God. Your spirit is recreated in Christ. However, did you also revoke the license you gave to satan, if you ever willingly served him through false religion?

The kind of idolatry I am talking about here is something all of us can agree on. Witchcraft, Mormonism, Jehovah's Witness, Wicca, News Age Cult, palm reading... it's a long list.

How about spiritual impartations you received from someone who was demonized? Crazy as it sounds, I have seen children of God looking up to a leader whose physical manifestation is misunderstood as the work of the Holy Spirit instead of the demon it is!

They crave the same manifestation thinking that it will draw them closer to God. They open themselves up wide to the influence. Asking for it. Praying for it, and so receiving it.

Spiritual Discernment Workshop

The point is, when you submit yourself to satan and worship him in any way, you give him possession. When someone who has been involved in the occult gets born again, it is essential to have them renounce that old contract!

I have seen this a lot in my lifetime because of the strong ancestral worship that is found in South Africa. Many are brought up worshipping the ancestors and demons. Getting born again is not enough – they have to renounce their old ways. If they do not do this, they will remain possessed and when things get tough, they will go to their witch doctors for cures.

If you grew up in a family that engaged in the occult, dealing with it is so simple. Rip up that old contract. You see, dealing with demons does not have to be all intense and all super duper.

So you gave him license. Well take it back! How hard is that? Never forget, God gave man a free will! What kind of staying power does satan have over someone he possesses?

Jesus died and His blood leaves a stain so strong that no demon in hell can counter it. What does satan have? He has only sin to keep us anchored. He has no blood to keep us. He has no power to sustain us, and the death he uses to bring fear was overthrown by Christ.

So no... satan does not have a permanent hold on any man! While Jesus could boast that no one could snatch us from His hand, satan has to reduce himself to guile and trickery to keep man serving him.

No matter what contract you made with satan, the only thing that keeps him anchored is sin. Well now... we are prophets... we know what to do with sin, don't we?

SEXUAL IMMORALITY

Why sexual immorality? Well just like the Word says, when you have sex with someone, you become one with them. In other words, you enter into a blood covenant with them. You yield your body up to them as a sheep to the slaughter.

We spoke in *Prophetic Warrior* about sexual abuse and sin. Sexual abuse most certainly leads to oppression. The spiritual link with the abuser causes your mind, emotions, and will to come under serious attack.

However, when you wake up one day and decide to engage in sexual debauchery for yourself, is the day that you offer your body to satan for his evil purpose. The moment you decided to have that homosexual affair, you worshipped satan with your body.

The moment you decided to sleep around, you offered your body up, through a covenant act, to the enemy. You gave him ownership.

Being attacked with thoughts of lust is oppression. Engaging in pornography and joining your body to someone you should not, leads to possession.

From there, it feels as if your body is not your own. You might not slither on the floor like a snake (although some have!) but lust will control you to the point of destroying your marriage.

You will lust after those you should not and struggle with every other work of the flesh. Your sin will feel uncontrollable... and what is the fruit? Satan is glorified in your broken marriage and torn relationships. You made a contract of blood and that possessing demon has ownership of you.

When trying to minister to someone with uncontrollable issues with lust, realize that you are dealing with possession. Deal with the sin. Deal with the demon. Help them gain the victory.

HATRED (ABUSIVE ANGER)

A child grows up seeing his father beat his mother. After years of taking the abuse himself, his mind is warped with a strange sense of how to deal with conflicts. He is oppressed by the enemy.

The day he chooses to raise his hand in hatred or in anger, he offers his body up willingly to what he knows is wrong. Have you ever seen anyone possessed with a demon of anger?

It is not the most pleasant experience - I can tell you! Personally, I do not think that "anger" is a strong enough word. I prefer the word "hate" because that is exactly what it looks like.

The Lord tells us to be angry and not to sin, but hate is something else all together. It is an uncontrollable anger that has been given over to the enemy. When you deliberately decide to use violence to solve your problems, you give your body up as a living sacrifice to the enemy.

You allow the hatred within to drive you, and as you do that, you give satan a place he should never have. Now you are trying to serve the Lord, and you find yourself doing things you should not.

You find yourself raising your hand in anger when you should not. You walk away ashamed, wishing that you had more self-control. Yes, you need self-control, but first you need to deal with that possessing demon!

It is a lot more than just bad judgment calls now. Perhaps it was a poor choice at the beginning. A deliberate sin that you chose to engage in that has now evolved to something else. Anger and bitterness turned to hatred, and you used that force to get your way and beat others down both physically and psychologically.

As you let this principle drive home, you become armed with yet another weapon of warfare.

Knowing the truth sets you free! If you are ministering to someone that is struggling with uncontrollable sin that seems to "take them over," you now know what you are dealing with! You are dealing with a possessing demon and you need to go back to the time that they gave it license.

DRUG USE (DRUNKENNESS)

I have yet to minister to anyone who took drugs and not have had to deal with demons. Taking narcotics or using alcohol to the point of becoming an alcoholic, delivers up their body to the enemy.

Not only do drugs help the user to enter into a spiritual state, but they are experiencing that state without Christ. They go in uncovered, and they go in having given their bodies to the enemy.

If you are ministering to someone who was a drug user, I promise, you have a possessing demon to deal with. Not only did they yield up their bodies, but their spirit as well through the experience.

MANIFESTATION OF OPPRESSION VS. POSSESSION

I am going to list just a few points on how to identify demonic oppression versus possession. It is quite obvious for the most part, but let us summarize what you have learned so far! Note that someone will not necessarily display all of the points at once. However, once you minister to them, it will be quite clear which category they fall into.

Oppression	Possession
• Attacks on the mind • Emotions out of control • Confusing thoughts • Struggle with fear and guilt • Sense of feeling overwhelmed • Nightmares • Inner striving and conflict	• Physical manifestations (demon might speak through person's lips) • Uncontrollable sinful actions • Uncontrollable anger • Uncontrollable lying • Uncontrollable lust

This chapter was taken from the book **Prophetic Counter Insurgence** written by Colette Toach.

SCRIPTURES TO MEMORIZE

Acts 10:38 How God anointed Jesus of Nazareth with the Holy Spirit and with power, who went about doing good and healing all who were oppressed by the devil, for God was with Him.

Luke 11:34 The lamp of the body is the eye. Therefore, when your eye is good, your whole body also is full of light. But when your eye is bad, your body also is full of darkness.

35 Therefore take heed that the light which is in you is not darkness.

1 Corinthians 10:20 Rather, that the things which the Gentiles sacrifice they sacrifice to demons and not to God, and I do not want you to have fellowship with demons.

21 You cannot drink the cup of the Lord and the cup of demons; you cannot partake of the Lord's table and of the table of demons.

KEY PRINCIPLES

- ✓ Doing warfare in the heavenly realm opens doors in the natural realm.
- ✓ Demonic oppression is the continual attack of the enemy that you eventually submit to.
- ✓ Demonic possession is the result of yielding your body up to the service and worship of satan.
- ✓ The doors that open you to demonic possession: sins of the flesh, Idolatry, sexual immorality, hatred and drug use.

PRACTICAL APPLICATION:

COMPLETE THE TABLE

Insert each of the following points under the correct heading in the table below

1. Uncontrollable lying
2. Attacks on the mind
3. Uncontrollable anger
4. Emotions out of control
5. Confusing thoughts
6. Physical manifestations (demon might speak through person's lips)
7. Struggle with fear and guilt
8. Uncontrollable sinful actions
9. Sense of feeling overwhelmed
10. Nightmares
11. Inner striving and conflict
12. Uncontrollable lust

Oppression	Possession
•	•
•	•
•	•
•	•
•	•
•	•

EXTRA NOTES

CHAPTER 09

SATAN'S KINGDOM – PRINCIPALITIES AND POWERS

Chapter 09 – Satan's Kingdom – Principalities and Powers

Chapter Reference: *Prophetic Warrior*, Chapter 2

"To know your enemy is to know yourself."

No quote could have said it better. It is when you understand how the enemy operates, that you come to appreciate the authority that you have been given in Christ.

There is nothing quite like looking over a battlefield, arrayed with troops as far as the eye can see, and to understand what you are facing. Then again, to see those troops be swept aside with just one breath from God helps you to understand what you have through the blood of Christ.

Now Apostle Paul – this is a general who knew his enemy, and was well versed in spiritual warfare at the highest level. There was no doubt in his mind who he was coming against, and exactly what that battlefield looked like.

He knew very well that we do not wrestle against flesh and blood! Consider this passage

> *Ephesians 6:12 For we wrestle not against flesh and blood, but against principalities, against powers, against the rulers of the darkness of this world, against spiritual wickedness in high [places]. (KJV)*

Outlined beautifully for us, this passage displays for us the ranks and structure of the enemy.

So when you see or sense something in the spirit, the Lord is trying to tell you exactly what level you are doing warfare at.

A demon is not just a demon! Just like an angel is not an angel. For example, you have the angel Michael who is the leader of the warrior angels. He leads the troops and because of that, carries more authority.

It is the same with demons. Do you see why I call the enemy a copycat? He just took what God had already put in place, and set up the competition. To be fair, it is all he knew! This helps us though to determine exactly what we are facing, and the level of faith we need to overcome.

As you continue increasing your prophetic authority, you will also see yourself being drawn into higher levels of spiritual warfare. It is why the Lord has challenged your faith so much.

It takes as much faith to bind a demon as it does to speak healing to a broken heart. It takes as much faith to dethrone satan in your life, as it does to believe a promise God has given to you.

> **KEY PRINCIPLE**
>
> What you sense in the spirit, is an indication of what kind and what level of warfare you are facing.

In fact, it just takes a mustard seed of faith to engage in spiritual warfare. You have a mustard seed don't you? Well then you are well able to deal with the pesky principality demon that lies at the lowest rank in satan's kingdom.

PRINCIPALITIES

> *Colossians 2:15 [And] having spoiled principalities and powers, he made a shew of them openly, triumphing over them in it. (KJV)*

Strong's Concordance Definition
746
arche {ar-khay'}

AV - beginning 40, principality 8, corner 2, first 2, misc. 6; 58

- beginning, origin
- the first place, principality, rule, magistracy
- of angels and demons

So these guys are the first in line. The first to be sent out - first to get shot. Some things are universal. There are scores of principality demons.

They cause mischief and cause things to be difficult for us. They are spirits of infirmity, confusion, and strife. Pesky demons that make walking out our calling a challenge. This scripture is a good picture of the kind of mess they make:

> *James 3:16 For where envy and self- seeking exist, confusion and every evil thing are there.*

In fact, they are so sneaky, that sometimes you can miss them in the chaos. You struggle with thoughts in your mind and fall into temptation. Well you can be sure that a little principality demon had a part to play in that – attacking your mind with ideas that were not of God.

An eruption of strife in your home, followed by frustration and a sense of being overwhelmed… yep you have a host of principalities having a heyday under your roof.

They serve the enemy by arranging circumstances and putting stumbling blocks in your road, with the intention to make you trip and fall. When you trip and open up to sin, that is when you give the enemy license and you can be sure that a power demon is standing by to take advantage of the opportunity.

Imagine the principality demon like a stone in your shoe. They make things uncomfortable. You do not realize something is a problem until you feel a bruise forming under your foot – causing you to stumble in your walk.

WHAT THEY LOOK LIKE IN THE SPIRIT

As in all things, when we see visions, they are a type and a shadow with a message to help us understand what we are facing. I do spiritual warfare at varied levels and when the Lord wants me to see what exactly I am dealing with, He shows me demons in various forms.

What I share here might be something that you have seen as well, but it also might be different. So with each of these types I am going to share briefly how I see this demonic category in the spirit, so if you see something similar in the future, you know what you are dealing with.

I see principality demons like insects most of the time. When praying for someone, I might see something in the spirit like a scorpion or worm –both of which have negative connotations in Scripture.

What I see, gives me an indication of the level of attack, and also the kind of attack it is.

HOW TO SPOT THEM

There are always telltale signs when a spirit of infirmity is at play. If someone is struggling with a sudden sickness that they cannot shake, no matter what they do, you can be sure that something demonic is involved.

You get sick with something and no amount of medication helps. You pray and it lifts for a bit, and then comes right on back! No one can seem to find the reason why you are sick! It just "is." Well I am not going into dealing with spirits of infirmity into much detail, but I am going to say this – they are just principality demons!

They are on the lowest rung of the ladder. Pawns. Foot soldiers. You have enough faith to bind a spirit of strife? Then you can also bind that spirit of infirmity!

POWERS

Strong's Concordance Definition
1849
exousia {ex-oo-see'-ah}

AV - power 69, authority 29, right 2, liberty 1, jurisdiction 1,

strength 1; 103

- the power of authority (influence) and of right (privilege)
- the power of rule or government (the power of him whose will
- and commands must be submitted to by others and obeyed)
- the power of judicial decisions
- jurisdiction
- one who possesses authority

Just like their name denotes, these are a higher level of demon that keep the principalities in check. They are an officer in satan's kingdom that sends out the troops to try and get a reaction out of you!

They co-ordinate the principalities for a defined attack. Without them, principalities would just run around in a hundred directions at once, each trying to bring about their own kind of chaos. The rulers make sure that the attack has focus.

> *KEY PRINCIPLE*
>
> A power demon is the one coordinating the principalities for a focused attack.

And so when the enemy is leveling a physical attack on you, he is going to get a couple of principalities to take a hold of you. Your attack begins with a cold, then somehow transforms into a stomach virus. From there, you also suffer from an allergy... you are left wondering what is going on!

It feels as if you start with one thing, and keep hopping from one to the next. You barely get your head up, only to find another wave coming against you.

Your finances are under attack. You get a bill in the mail for a parking ticket. You pay it. You barely get over that and something breaks in your house, so you have to give that money out again. It seems that every little principality demon of theft is on your back.

Now you could spend the whole day dealing with this demon and that... or just get the guy that is coordinating it all. That would be the power demon.

WHAT THEY LOOK LIKE

I see these demons in the spirit like large animals. For someone that is under bondage to a spirit of anger, I see it like an angry gorilla with its teeth bared. I might even see a viper with poison under its tongue.

When I see this, then I know what I am dealing with! Bitterness is the license given and the result is uncontrollable anger and malice.

I have seen a power demon of theft like a ravenous wolf seeking to steal, kill, or destroy. I see a power demon of divination like a python – seeking to squeeze the life out of his victim.

I see the spirit of deception as serpents as well. Fitting if you consider their nature!

The good news? Power demons know your authority in Christ probably better than you do! They know that when you stand in Christ, that they have to let go. I have had little struggle with power demons. Once they are manifest and their license is removed, they do not hang around.

HOW TO SPOT THEM

They are identified by a continuous attack in a focused direction. You do not get hit with just one sickness... but one after the other! Not just one thing is stolen, but many of them!

It is this continuity that defines this kind of demon. You break one glass and you are just being clumsy! You break a glass, crash your car, twist your ankle and hit your head on the open kitchen cabinet... and you have a power demon of destruction with his crosshairs on you!

There are times when we do not take care of our bodies and allow our immune system to drop. You just feel like sleeping and taking it easy. Yes, weariness is not a sign of blessing, but sometimes it is your body's way of forcing you to rest.

You do not exercise and you put on weight. Yes, when it is out of control, the enemy could certainly be playing a part. However, if a bit of exercise brings it into balance again, it is not a demon to blame for that entire box of cookies you ate in your moment of depression!

However, if you are suffering from weight gain, hair loss, anemia, and your hormones are not coming in line no matter what you do… you have a power demon pulling the strings by setting those principalities to work in synchronous harmony.

This chapter was taken from the book *Prophetic Warrior* written by Colette Toach.

SCRIPTURES TO MEMORIZE

Ephesians 6:12 For we wrestle not against flesh and blood, but against principalities, against powers, against the rulers of the darkness of this world, against spiritual wickedness in high [places]. (KJV)

Ephesians 1:17 Colossians 2:15 [And] having spoiled principalities and powers, he made a shew of them openly, triumphing over them in it. (KJV)

James 3:16 For where envy and self-seeking exist, confusion and every evil thing are there.

KEY PRINCIPLES

- ✓ What you sense in the spirit, is an indication of what kind and what level of warfare you are facing.
- ✓ Principalities are the lowest level of demon, first level of attack
- ✓ A power demon is the one coordinating the principalities for a focused attack.

PRACTICAL APPLICATION:

1. **DRILLING THROUGH ROCK - LOOKING AT THE BLOCKAGES IN YOUR LIFE.**

    Take a look at your life and make a list of the things you are struggling to get a breakthrough with right now.

    Answer these questions:

    a. Is this struggle or problem a blessing from the Lord?
    b. Am I feeling guilty or full of fear as I tackle this problem?
    c. Is this a test that I am expected to pass?
    d. Is this situation of the Lord, or of the enemy?

Struggling With	Is it a blessing from the Lord?	Do you feel guilt or fear?	Is it a test to pass?	Is it of the Lord or the enemy?

EXTRA NOTES

CHAPTER 10

SATAN'S KINGDOM – RULERS AND PRINCES

Chapter 10 – Satan's Kingdom – Rulers and Princes

Chapter Reference: *Prophetic Warrior*, Chapter 3

Now we are getting down and dirty. The first two levels of demons cause us to stub our spiritual toes and open our mouths to say things we would not. You sit in bed, sick for days on end and I challenge you not to bite the head off the next person who asks you if you are feeling better yet!

"No! I am not feeling better! Now would you just leave me alone while I sit here and feel sorry for myself…"

After one financial attack after the other, it does not take much to spark of strife in your home. "What do you mean that you need more money for clothes? Can't you see I am working hard here? Can't you see what I have to deal with?"

That is their purpose. To bring you to a point of exasperation. To bring you to a point where you start seeking out solutions for your problem that do not include Christ. You pray for money and get no answers.

You pray for healing and nothing happens. So you go to the world. You start searching. Before you know it, you are looking in places you should not to meet your needs and you can be sure that a good looking ruler demon is standing by to lead you the rest of the way.

RULERS

Strong's Concordance Definition
2888

AV - ruler 1; 1

1) lord of the world, prince of this age
1a) the devil and his demons

This is how generational curses originate. Someone starts searching for spiritual answers outside of Christ. There is only one way to the Father, and it is through Christ.

There is only one way to navigate the realm of the spirit safely, and that is while wearing as a mantle, the blood of Jesus. Now what happens when you decide to take a trip into the realm of the spirit without the blood to shield you?

Well a good example of that is king Saul who decided to seek out a medium for answers instead of the Lord. He paid for that with his life. He conjured up a spirit who the witch said was Elijah. In a matter of days, he and his son were dead.

The Lord is not to be trifled with, and when you try to gain access to the realm of the spirit outside of the blood of Christ, you do so unguarded. You open yourself up to ruler demons that are ready to help you have such a spiritual experience.

> *2 Corinthians 11:14 And no wonder! For Satan himself transforms himself into an angel of light.*
> *15 Therefore it is no great thing if his ministers also transform themselves into ministers of righteousness, whose end will be according to their works.*

The angel of light will come to tempt you, but you do not need to entertain him! If you do though, you open a door in the spirit that leaves your back open. This is where demon possession originates. It is one thing to be under attack from power demons, it is another to allow a spiritual experience outside of Christ.

KEY PRINCIPLE

When someone has sought spiritual solutions outside of Christ, their spirit is contaminated by a ruler demon.

That is why when someone has been involved in the occult or false religion, you can be sure that there is a ruler demon that is involved. This is also true for people who were heavy drug users.

What is the purpose of taking drugs, other than to heighten the senses and to give them a spiritual experience? This experience, having been done outside of Christ, allows a demonic spiritual influence entry into their lives.

When someone has sought spiritual solutions outside of Christ, their spirit is contaminated by a ruler demon. When they are unsaved, it takes over and we will talk about that more when I teach you about helping someone who is demonized.

For now, realize that when someone gets saved, that their spirit is renewed! That ruler demon's influence is limited, and "hangs out" on the outside of their spirits, however it still has influence enough to lead them astray. Consider Simon, the sorcerer that Peter rebuked harshly in Act 8:23.

He may have been born again, but his sin and "spiritual searching" out of Christ left him bound.

BEELZEBUB

When a ruler demon is in play, you have a demonic prince that has a greater level of authority. Beelzebub is a good picture of this kind of demon, as outlined in the passage below.

> *Luke 11:19 And if I cast out demons by Beelzebub, by whom do your sons cast them out? Therefore, they will be your judges.*
> *20 But if I cast out demons with the finger of God, surely the kingdom of God has come upon you.*
> *21 When a strong man, fully armed, guards his own palace, his goods are in peace:*

Sometimes such a demon can be called a "strong man" demon or a possessing demon. Different ministries have given them names, but they all fall under the same category of "Ruler." Each ruler will have a specific realm of influence.

WHAT THEY LOOK LIKE

I see these demons in the spirit with more humanlike characteristics. For example, I had a dream once of Beelzebub when I was confronted with the New Age cult (I shared about this in the *Prophetic Functions* book). I saw him as a mix between a human and insect. It was not pleasant!

I have seen the occult demon as humanoid but more like the typical picture you see of the devil in traditional artwork. I see an occult demon having a forked tongue. When I see this demon, I know that the person I am ministering to was involved in some form of false religion or spiritual act.

It does not surprise me then to find out that a past mentor was a heretic or that they once dabbled in spiritual matters outside of Christ.

I see the jezebel spirit like an old witch. When I see that in the spirit, I know what I am dealing with and how to handle it.

In the chapters that follow I will teach you about how these gain license, but there is one point I want to make clear here.

When someone has been bound by such a demon for long periods of time, you can be sure that it has helped shaped their character. It is for this reason, that dealing with ruler demons can be a challenge.

It is no longer a case of just casting out a demon. Deliverance needs to be two-fold. Firstly, you need to deal with the demon, but then you will also need to deal with the character that has been formed in the person through this influence!

HOW TO SPOT THEM

This demon is most often exposed when someone manifests in the middle of a meeting! However, you will also see it through habitual, uncontrollable sin.

The spirit of death is another. This is a demon that seeks to destroy this life that God has given to us. Cancer, HIV and other diseases fall under his influences. When you see someone that continually struggles with terminal illness, you can be sure that a ruler is involved.

Uncontrollable sin and lying is another indication of this level of demon being present. We all make sinful choices, but there are those that find it that much harder. A ruler demon of lust, for example, manifests itself through addiction to pornography.

While a deep psychological need might have led the person to seek out a "deep experience" in something not of God, once that demon has a hold, they find that they "cannot" stop.

BUILDER OF STRONGHOLDS

Now there is no such thing as a victim! They can most definitely "stop" with the help of Christ! However, with someone bound by a ruler demon, it makes it very difficult. Everything in them craves to do what the demon wants them to crave.

For someone with a jezebel spirit, no matter how much they know that they need to step aside and not control, they feel pushed to take action. They even feel that it is justified!

They are indeed, the builders of the strongholds in our lives. They have built strongholds and have gained their power through choices we have made throughout our lives. I teach in *The Stain of Sin – Overcoming Curses* message that generational curses are derived from repeated, unrepeated sin. This is the ruler demon's playground.

> *KEY PRINCIPLE*
>
> Ruler demons are the builders of strongholds in our minds and hearts through the choices we have made.

Now like I said, just dealing with the demon is not enough in these cases. You have to rebuild the home that the demon lived in! This influence has conditioned their thinking and often the danger lies in that they think the "pushiness" is of the Lord!

Mix that with someone who is spirit-filled and you have quite a mess. Because they tapped into a spirit that was either contaminated or outside of Christ, they receive an angel of light into their lives.

Then they get spirit-filled, and the Holy Spirit begins to influence them as well. It is glorious! Did you really think that satan would say, "No problem! You want to leave my camp in favor of God's? Sure! Have a blast!?"

Hardly. He will begin with confusion and just "add" to what God tells you. Why steal the revelation when he can just contaminate it with a mixed message? Why try to stop you from running, when he can make you run harder… in the wrong direction?

This is the danger of a ruler demon and one that you will come into confrontation with more than once in yourself and in others. A straight out deception from the enemy is often easy to spot. What is difficult is when a true message from God is mixed in with the handiwork of a ruler demon!

SOLUTIONS

So what are you to do? When I faced this situation in my life, I was devastated! The Lord made it easy for me and told me to put the whole lot on the altar. My revelations, my call… everything.

He told me to even put down what I knew was from Him. I laid it on the altar and He said to me, "Now stand back… "

In the spirit I saw a ball of fire fall from heaven and consume what I had put on the altar. Once the smoke cleared I stepped forward and saw something amazing. Where my "revelations" were contaminated, they lay as ash on that altar. However, the ones that were truly of God now gleamed in the sunlight, as pure gold!

The Lord told me that day, that I never had to be afraid to put anything on the altar that I was unsure of, because when I let go and allowed the fire to come, that what was gold would only be refined that much more.

Identifying the work of satan in your life is half of the battle. When you can see him, then you can drag him into the street to get shot! The greatest enemy though is not the one that comes like a roaring lion, but the one that comes like a wolf in sheep's clothing.

The ruler demon is such a character. He is a possessing demon that has not only brought with it a skill and power to help the person in bondage, but also used that influence to shape their lives.

Never think that people just want to get rid of their demons. There is more that a ruler demon does than just lead them away from Christ.

He also gives them power. Do you think that Simon the Sorcerer was kidding when he asked to pay for the Holy Spirit? What do you think he did before being saved? He had real power!

He had the kind of power that the priests of Pharaoh had that turned their staffs into serpents! This kind of demon gives the person who invites it a sense of peace. That demon of lust brings gratification in the moment that it is entertained, with the aftertaste of guilt.

And so like a drug, the person will take it again and again! The jezebel spirit gives the person a sense of power and control. Broken relationships follow.

Beelzebub gives a person a spiritual superiority and sense of control over their lives. Temporal values? An ability to create wealth. Do not be fooled into thinking that demons just bring evil. It is the "good" that they give that lures people into their trap.

Do not lose hope though. You serve a King that has a trick or two up his sleeve! He has the power to shine a light into the darkness and to expose every true intention. He can separate the sheep from the goats, and burn off the tares, showing us the wheat.

DEMON POSSESSION: BELIEVER VS. UNBELIEVER

I am going to make mention of an important point very briefly here. (I will be going into further detail in the next book in the series.) There is a distinct difference in how you deal with a demon of this category in a believer and unbeliever.

You will see so many accounts of an unbeliever being possessed with such a demon. You have the man at the tombs that Jesus set free. You have Mary Magdalene that He also set free. So it is quite a stark contrast when Simon the Sorcerer is so strongly corrected by Peter.

It is clear that Simon was demonized and even history teaches us that he started a sect that stood against the truth of the Gospel. Yet Peter did not cast the possessing demon out of him. Instead he told him to, "Repent!" This is a powerful principle!

A blood bought child of God has every authority in the name of Christ to tell any demon to flee – especially one that they gave license to. When someone is unsaved, they do not have this authority. So if an unbeliever manifests a demon, you can tell it to be silent and deal with it accordingly.

However, if a believer manifests, it is essential that you talk to the person and get them to their right mind. Once they are able to take control again, you can instruct them on how to deal with the license that they gave the enemy. They have every authority to pray, "I revoke the license that you have given to me! Satan you will loose your hold right now!"

KEY PRINCIPLE

A believer has every authority to tell a demon to leave and cannot be "possessed."

I have seen deliverance done like this in the lives of many believers and can truly say that it is powerful! Not only that, but because of the rest that it is done in, the person gains a greater conviction and has less of a chance of allowing that demon access again. They take responsibility for their sin. They take responsibility for taking the license away. They take responsibility to walk out their own call in fear and trembling!

So if you are faced with someone in bondage to a ruler demon, let me say this – yes you have some work ahead of you. However never get so wrapped up in the strength of the demon, that you forget the power of God.

The Holy Spirit is well able to arm you with the anointing to break that yoke and to rip the mask off the enemy to expose the ugly monster he really is. Above all, Jesus is our mighty general leading us into battle. He has never lost a war. He has never lost a soldier and He is not about to start now!

WICKEDNESS IN HIGH PLACES - PRINCES

Strong's Concordance Definition
2032
epouranios {ep-oo-ran'-ee-os}

AV - heavenly 16, celestial 2, in heaven 1, high 1; 20

1) existing in heaven
1a) things that take place in heaven
1b) the heavenly regions
1b1) heaven itself, the abode of God and angels
1b2) the lower heavens, of the stars
1c) the heavenly temple or sanctuary

> *Ephesians 2:2 In which you once walked according to the course of this world, according to the prince of the power of the air, the spirit who now works in the sons of disobedience,*
> *3 among whom also we all once conducted ourselves in the lusts of our flesh, fulfilling the desires of the flesh and of the mind, and were by nature children of wrath, just as the others.*

The top dogs! Just like in the natural, these are the generals of darkness. These are not possessing demons – but they are too happy to arrange a meeting with one if they can!

The wickedness in high places (or princes as I like to call them) rule over a lot more than just the demons that they control. Their main purpose is to rule the systems of the world. Each is in control of a very specific realm.

That is what Paul is talking about here in Ephesians 2:2. He says that in times past we walked according to the "course of this world according to the prince of the authority of the air."

In other words, when we were still citizens of satan's kingdom, we walked under the bondage of the systems of the world – systems that are controlled by the princes of the air!

PRINCES OF SYSTEMS

They coordinate and arrange entire structures to help them fulfill their purpose.

This is where you will find your territorial spirits. You will have princes with varied influences.

To name a few of them: family generational princes, territorial princes, and princes who are in control of specific archetypes.

What separates them from the other categories, is that they build the structure in which the other demons can fulfill their purpose.

You will learn that the greatest warfare you will face will be as the systems of the world try to dominate and crush the work of the Lord. Even today, you will see ministries being crippled by financial or political attack. That is what John was talking about here:

> *1 John 2:15 Love not the world, neither the things [that are] in the world. If any man loves the world, the love of the Father is not in him. (KJV)*

Well who do you think is pulling the strings behind those systems? Now the systems in the world have been set in place by man, but the princes of the air have had a heavy hand in shaping them according to their will.

KEY PRINCIPLE

"Princes" rule over the systems of the world. They coordinate and arrange structures in their specific realms.

So with the organized structure in place, you will find that they create the environment in this world for the other demons to perform the other tasks I have already mentioned.

For example, for a power demon to keep attacking you with financial loss, you can be sure that it is the financial system of this world that was the structure in which that demon worked!

Paul faced attacks from the political system of his day. A system that satan used time and again to cripple his ministry. Suddenly his words, "we wrestle not with flesh and blood..." is illuminated.

He realized that it was not a worldly magistrate or king that he was doing warfare against. Rather he was wrestling with the prince of that political system that had established the structure for that attack.

To overcome and to relieve that pressure, his warfare was not to be done against that king or magistrate. Rather, he had to take his warfare into the heavenly realm and dethrone that prince controlling the whole thing.

How often have you engaged in spiritual warfare, binding people? You bind your landlord for giving you a hard time. You bind your boss for being used of the devil. If you want to see real victory in your life, then you need to take your warfare a little higher than that. You need to bind the prince that is controlling the system through which that pressure is coming.

We are now starting to settle on the level of warfare that you are called to as a prophet. I have given you a picture of what satan's kingdom looks like, but it is in this realm that you start finding your inner warrior!

God has called you to do warfare at the highest level, and this moves past just dealing with a principality or two.

Your job is not just about dealing with demons in people. Your job is to go to the princes that have set things in place.

WHAT THEY LOOK LIKE

Princes are pretty boys. Lucifer himself was called the Star of the morning. The fact that I see them in this way is fitting, because of the lure that they have on mankind. They entice, seduce and invite mankind to follow after them.

When I see the prince of lust (the one in control of the pornographic system of this world) I see him as rather feminine and attractive. He is flamboyant wearing many different colored clothing. Overdone, just like the system he has instituted in the world.

When I see territorial princes they often resemble the bondage in the country. As for Lucifer, do not think that he looks like an evil warlock with horns. Keep in mind that he stood next to the Father in the Heavenly Kingdom.

> *KEY PRINCIPLE*
>
> Your job is not just about dealing with demons in people.
> Your job is to go to the princes that have set things in place.

A prince I saw recently was one over an Asian family generation. I was ministering to one of my disciples who was having such a struggle with generational curses. When we prayed, I saw the "prince of her family" that had been given license from generation to generation.

Not only was he the bringer of the curses in their family but was also responsible for creating the archetype and mindset that was prevalent in that family culture.

HOW TO SPOT THEM

When you start looking past your daily struggles and towards the systems that are involved in bearing down on you, you easily identify the princes of air at work. Sudden external attacks that come on a church or pressure to conform to an archetype – all the workings of a prince.

For most believers, they will likely do warfare with principalities, powers and rulers.

Although every believer has the authority to bind any demon, they will not be called of God to deal with the princes of the air, unless there is a specific attack levied against them.

The rules change for you as a prophet. You will spend more time doing higher levels of warfare than ever before. It is for you to decree and intercede so that the structures of satan can be destroyed so that people can be set free!

So if the Lord has had you trying to deal with the religious system in the world so that His people can see clearly, then you are right on track. Do not try to bind the pastor that is not teaching according to what you feel is accurate. Look higher! There is a lot more here than meets the eye.

You are battling a prince of the air that has set his structure in place for some time now. There are varied levels of princes, and at the very top, you have what we call the Counsel of Wickedness that rule them all. Are you fighting laws that are restricting the church? You are not fighting the President – you are fighting the prince residing over your country.

It is time that you allow the Holy Spirit to condition you with "eyes to see" and "ears to hear" as a prophetic warrior. Lift your eyes higher! Look up and see that your place is not in casting down the rulers of this world, but the rulers of the air that keep putting people in place that they want.

Consider Persia that was as evil as it came. Yet in the middle of their rule, the Lord raised up Esther and Mordecai on behalf of His people.

Consider Daniel who did warfare and repented on behalf of Israel. He did not bind kings, but simply decreed into the earth what God wanted. This warfare did more than any weapon of natural warfare.

COUNSEL OF WICKEDNESS

As you begin to engage in this warfare, sooner or later you are going to bump into specific powers of the air that we call the Counsel of Wickedness. Later on we will go a bit more into them, but together they rule everything else.

You already know that the princes control different systems, but there are some systems outlined in scripture that we see trending throughout the Old and New Testaments.

These are systems that satan has used throughout the generations to tear down the Church, and to make sure his plan is established. I am going to deal with the three that you are going to face the most in your prophetic training.

LUCIFER

> *Matthew 4:9 And he said to Him, All these things I will give You if You will fall down and worship me.*
> *10 Then Jesus said to him, Away with you, Satan! For it is written, 'You shall worship the Lord your God, and Him only you shall serve...*

Lucifer being the king of deception, heads the religious systems of the world. Always craving the worship that was God's, he gathers those around himself that can praise his name.

When you look at the attack on Christians in so many nations, you see the work of satan. You see how he pushes his agenda in every false religion, while trying to silence the voice of Christianity.

Having done this for so many years, you would think that he would be used to the fact that each time he tries, that he gets a serious whipping. He is still smarting from the big stick that Jesus beat Him with on Calvary - a stick that we have been using since then.

Yet, I guess if there is one quality that is not pure evil that satan has... it is hope. He is deluded into hoping that he can win a war he already lost. Well leave him to his self-inflicted deception, because while he is running around with his propaganda, we are getting armed for the greatest revival this world has ever seen!

APOLLYON

Abaddon {ab-ad-dohn'} = 'destruction'

1) ruin
2) destruction

3) the place of destruction
4) the name of the angel-prince of the infernal regions, the minister of death and the author of havoc on the earth

> *Revelation 9:10 They had tails like scorpions, and there were stings in their tails. Their power was to hurt men five months.*
> *11 And they had as king over them the angel of the bottomless pit, whose name in Hebrew is Abaddon, but in Greek he has the name Apollyon.*

Apollyon – one of satan's generals that takes great delight in destroying the bodies that God has given to us. He heads up the medical system of this world and when he has his way, does his utmost to keep us reminded that there is no healing in Christ – only through his own touch.

Not only is he the one who rules over all the physical attack that we face from the enemy again and again, he is the one who will keep you bound with medical bills, dependence on drugs, and chained with fear.

He warps the good that God has put in man. Man is by nature hungry to learn and keen to adventure into the unknown. God has put it in us to preserve the bodies that He has given to us. Taking this natural desire, Apollyon has used it to his own advantage.

Having battles with insurance, hospitals, medication, sickness, and fear about dying? You are facing Apollyon. Bind him, and you will start seeing the Lord work through those same systems to bring you the blessing that He intended.

I am not one that subscribes to the medical industry as being "the devil," but I will say that Apollyon has played a heavy hand in it, to control who gets what. If he can condition your mind into believing "there is no hope for recovery," then his system did its job effectively.

PHARAOH

> *Ezekiel 31:17 They also went down to hell with it, with those slain by the sword; and those who were its strong arm dwelt in its shadows among the nations.*
> *18 'To which of the trees in Eden will you then be likened in glory and greatness? Yet you shall be brought down with the trees of Eden to the depths of the earth; you shall lie in the midst of the uncircumcised, with those slain by the sword. This is Pharaoh and all his multitude,' says the Lord God*

Pharaoh, is in charge of the financial system of this world. Taxes suddenly levied against you out of the blue? How about that sudden bill that was not anticipated? He uses the financial systems of the world to try and derail the Church.

Now I am saying "try" because I have found that when I do spiritual warfare at this level, I always see results! He might try to control the systems, but I have seen the Lord pass many a blessing to His people right from under his nose!

> *KEY PRINCIPLE*
>
> The Council of Wickedness: Lucifer – the religious system, Apollyon – the medical system, Pharaoh – the financial system.

Just like his namesake in the day of Joseph, I see the Lord raising up His people into positions of power, right under Pharaoh's nose! When you realize that it is Pharaoh that continues to hold onto the purse strings of the Church, you understand where you should be aiming your poison dart.

PRINCIPALITIES, POWERS, RULERS, PRINCES

The battlefield is set in array. The principalities are biting at the bit to be let loose. The powers are focusing their attack on one person at a time. The rulers have gained their license and are building strongholds with catapults that are hammering the castle walls.

Above them all, the princes of the air pull the strings on each system, helping create a sense of overwhelming defeat on their enemy.

This is your battlefield.

And this is your weapon.

> *Philippians 2:10 that at the name of Jesus every knee should bow, of those in heaven, and of those on earth, and of those under the earth,*

As the arrows fly and a deafening cheer rises up from satan's camp, the victory shout is cut short by the violent explosion of an atom bomb in their midst. The battle has begun, and with just one shout of the name of Jesus, a thousand demons are sent flying.

Another devastating eruption is seen, taking out a few princes and no less than 10,000 foot soldiers. That is what it looks like when two of you join your hearts in prayer.

> **KEY PRINCIPLE**
>
> Know your enemy, but more importantly know yourself.

It is easy to get sidetracked when you look at the massive army the enemy has put into array. It is easy to forget that you have a weapon of mass destruction - an atomic bomb of power that renders their arrows, poison, and evil intent, useless. Jesus Christ, the author of our faith. He is the source of all power.

Know your enemy – but more importantly know yourself. The previous book in this series was called *Prophetic Boot Camp*, for obvious reasons. You have been trained for a purpose, and now it is time for you to begin using some of what you have learned.

You have been stripped of your own ideas. You have been armed with the grace of Christ. Now all that is left, is for you to step out as a warrior.

This chapter was taken from the book **Prophetic Warrior** written by Colette Toach.

SCRIPTURES TO MEMORIZE

1 John 2:15 *Love not the world, neither the things [that are] in the world. If any man loves the world, the love of the Father is not in him. (KJV)*

Philippians 2:10 *that at the name of Jesus every knee should bow, of those in heaven, and of those on earth, and of those under the earth,*

Matthew 4:9 *And he said to Him, All these things I will give You if You will fall down and worship me.*

10 Then Jesus said to him, Away with you, Satan! For it is written, 'You shall worship the Lord your God, and Him only you shall serve...

KEY PRINCIPLES

- ✓ Ruler demons are the builders of strongholds in our minds and hearts through the choices we have made.
- ✓ Princes rule over the systems of the world. They coordinate and arrange structures in their specific realms.
- ✓ The Council of Wickedness: Lucifer – the religious system, Apollyon – the medical system, Pharaoh – the financial system.

Chapter 10

PRACTICAL APPLICATION:

MATCH THE COLUMNS:

In chapter 2 and 3 of the *Prophetic Warrior* book you learned about the structure of satan's kingdom. Taking the hierarchy of demons on your left, match them to their characteristics on the right.

Hierarchy	Matching Characteristics
1. Principality Demons 2. Power Demons 3. Ruler Demons 4. Princes of the Air	a. In charge of systems b. Look like insects in the spirit c. Builder of strongholds d. Possessing demon e. Look like animals in the spirit f. Continuous attack in a focused direction g. Humanlike characteristics h. Focuses the attack of lowest level demons i. Counsel of Wickedness j. The lowest level of demon k. Territorial l. Spirit of infirmity

THE STRUCTURE OF SATAN'S KINGDOM - WORD SEARCH:

Search Horizontal, Diagonal, Vertical and Backwards

C	Y	O	L	I	L	J	J	T	V	K	P	B	P	T
L	I	T	L	U	Y	O	H	O	S	R	B	U	H	M
S	Z	R	I	A	S	L	X	S	I	G	W	B	A	U
D	S	Q	C	M	E	T	B	N	X	H	O	E	R	W
Q	O	Y	F	U	R	C	C	Q	V	S	R	Z	A	B
L	W	T	S	E	M	I	N	U	A	V	L	L	O	T
D	F	A	W	T	P	S	F	I	H	M	D	E	H	L
O	E	O	L	A	E	X	T	N	R	M	S	E	F	S
E	P	T	L	V	A	M	L	A	I	P	Y	B	E	S
E	M	I	N	D	S	M	S	Q	N	I	S	R	A	R
O	T	G	K	I	V	F	G	U	Q	C	T	E	R	J
Y	C	I	W	K	H	C	X	M	R	M	E	L	K	J
D	L	E	I	F	E	L	T	T	A	B	M	U	C	A
A	P	O	L	L	Y	O	N	N	C	A	S	R	L	W
J	J	R	E	F	I	C	U	L	A	L	V	S	E	X

APOLLYON   BATTLEFIELD   BEELZEBUB   CIRCUMSTANCE   FEAR   INFIRMITY   MIND
LUCIFER   LUST   PHARAOH   POWER   PRINCE   PRINCIPALITY   RULER   SYSTEMS

EXTRA NOTES

CHAPTER 11

THE DIFFERENCE BETWEEN CURSES AND SPIRITUAL WARFARE

Chapter 11 – The Difference Between Curses and Spiritual Warfare

Chapter Reference: *Strategies of War*, Chapter 4

I am going to look very quickly at the difference between curses and spiritual warfare. I put this in because it is valid for those that are saying, "If everything is a curse, then when does spiritual warfare come in?"

THE ARROWS - A PICTURE OF SPIRITUAL WARFARE

This also confused me. Now, remember when I shared with you the picture of the city and the walls? I told you that the hole in the wall is a symbol of the curse. Well, arrows are a symbol of spiritual warfare.

Spiritual warfare is the external attack of the enemy. That is when people pray against you, speak against you, and the enemy decides to wear you down and accuse you in order to make that wall crumble and crack.

What the enemy is really trying to do is to get you to sin. Spiritual warfare has one intention. It is to get you to allow a hole in your wall. However, the scripture says that we need to stand with a shield of faith.

When those attacks come against you, the enemy comes with his lies and accusations, and all the hordes of hell are loosed against you, you do not have to be afraid.

You just stand with the shield of faith and say, "No. I am not succumbing to fear, bitterness, or any of this. I stand in the name of Jesus and I send back those arrows. They are not coming anywhere near my wall."

> ***Proverbs 25:28*** *Whoever has no rule over his own spirit is like a city broken down, without walls*

THE CRACK IN THE WALL - YOUR PERSONAL SIN

Yet, what if someone is speaking against you and you get bitter at them? You just dug yourself a hole in your wall, did you not? All those words and those curses that they are speaking over you are going to have an effect.

> ***Proverbs 26:2*** *Like a flitting sparrow, like a flying swallow, so a curse without cause shall not alight*

When you "give that curse a cause" it will strike you. Those arrows are going to get through your wall, if you allow yourself to fall into sin, to be bitter, angry, or frustrated. Spiritual warfare is all about satan trying to trip you up. You do not need to partake of the curses of others – just do not give that curse any cause. Spiritual warfare tries to trick you into giving that curse a cause (through sin)!

Is that not what he did in the Garden of Eden to trick Eve? He threw those arrows at her, but it was only when she ate the fruit that she sinned. That is what spiritual warfare is. It is warfare coming against you to get you to fail. That is why the Scripture says to bless and not curse.

It says in Romans 12:14,

Bless those who persecute you; bless and do not curse

So, how do you overcome spiritual warfare? You bless! You send those arrows back in the name of Jesus and you speak forth the blessing of God and make sure that there are no little holes, ditches, or cracks in that wall for those arrows to get through.

You say, "In the name of Jesus, I stand against those words and I speak faith, hope, and love. I will not be moved. This heart will not be affected by those words. This soul will not be discouraged because of what they said."

The minute it does, you allow those arrows to get in. When you allow those arrows into your life that is when they will destroy you. However, you do not have to experience this. That is the biggest difference between spiritual warfare and curses.

Spiritual warfare is the attack that comes from without, it is the arrow sent by the enemy through his agents that are only too willing to speak those words. In other words, if someone is praying against you, their prayers have no power, unless you allow them to.

You allow that power by getting bitter and frustrated at them. All you need to do is stand behind that shield of faith and remain in the spirit and in His blood, and those arrows will not touch you.

The scripture above in Proverbs 26 says that the curse will not alight. It will not have any power over you. He has delivered you from every curse, the curse of the people, the curse of their words. They cannot touch you... if you remain in Christ.

NO NEED TO FEAR

Does that not set you free? We have it backwards. I have people always travailing about, "This person is speaking a curse on me, putting voodoo and witchcraft on me and another person is praying against me."

Who cares? They cannot touch me. I am a blood-bought child of God. Check it out. The blood of Christ is all over me. You can't touch this! Christ did not die in vain. Yet, we sure act like it sometimes.

"I am so afraid that someone is going to put a curse on me…"

Give me your best shot. Check out what happens when you try to curse me. I do not need to deal with you because God has it under control.

> **Genesis 12:3** *I will bless those who bless you, and I will curse him who curses you; and in you all the families of the earth shall be blessed*

He said that He would bless those that bless me and curse those that curse me. You are not just coming against me. So, if you want to curse me, bring it on. That curse will bounce right back at you because God Himself will take that arrow and pierce it into your own heart.

So please, knock yourself out. I am not going to sit and travail over every single person that prays against this ministry because I do not need to. By cursing me, they sin and in their sin they undo themselves.

Why do I need to fret about it? What I do need to fret about is my own heart. I need to make sure that I do not get all stressed and bitter. "I am such a nice person. How could they say that?"

You just let that arrow through. You succumbed to the temptation and now you will experience that warfare at a whole new level. I hope that set you free because satan has been getting in, but not in the places that you think.

The place that you left unattended is where he is actually sneaking through. I have two simple definitions that I want to share with you here:

Curses – the fruit of un-repented, repetitive sin.

Spiritual Warfare – an onslaught of the enemy designed to discourage you and make you sin.

We have an answer for both of those and they both begin and end with the blood of Christ.

This chapter was taken from the book *Strategies of War* written by Colette Toach.

SCRIPTURES TO MEMORIZE

Ezra 2:63 And the governor said to them that they should not eat of the most holy things till a priest could consult with the Urim and Thummim.

Romans 12:14 Bless those who persecute you; bless and do not curse 18 the eyes of your understanding being enlightened; that you may know what is the hope of His calling, what are the riches of the glory of His inheritance in the saints,

Genesis 12:3 I will bless those who bless you, and I will curse him who curses you; and in you all the families of the earth shall be blessed

KEY PRINCIPLES

- ✓ **Curses** – the fruit of un-repented, repetitive sin.
- ✓ **Spiritual Warfare** – an onslaught of the enemy designed to discourage you and make you sin.
- ✓ Overcome spiritual warfare by responding with blessing.

PRACTICAL APPLICATION:

Have a close look at the personal sin in your life and apply the following steps.

STEP 1: GO BACK TO THE BEGINNING AND REPENT

1. Identify the sin that keeps establishing the curse in your life. Now, go back to the very first time you made that decision to react in sin. Perhaps the sin is rebellion.

    Go back to the very first time you took a stand and chose to respond in rebellion. Instead of submitting to authority, perhaps to your father, who accused you unjustly, let's say you responded in rebellion. Now you respond that way to authority all of the time. It is for you to go back to the first time you reacted in sin and to repent. Don't forget to take back the enemy's license, okay!

STEP 2: CHANGE YOUR HABITS

1. The most effective way to change that sinful response is to make the right decision in the heat of the moment.

   This is going to be a matter of identifying that moment when it is upon you and then choosing to respond righteously in that moment. Depending on how deeply rooted this habit is and how much demonic activity has been given license because of it, will make the habit easier or harder to uproot.

   I will not sugarcoat it. This may be difficult, especially if there is a demon involved.

It may be difficult, but it is not impossible. You are not a victim and you are free to choose the Lord's righteousness. If you are sick enough of the curses in your life, then will do what you need to do, to break free. The moment will come when it feels the most unfair. The circumstance will come when you least expect it.

If it is the sin of rebellion that you battle with, He will bring you the most unjust, controlling and undeserving leader that is around and the Lord will ask you to submit and honor him. He will use your spouse, who is the very one who inflicted the hurts of betrayal, and He will ask you to follow their lead and bend to their will. You will have the opportunity, in this moment, to reach out to your old familiar friend, or to reach out to Jesus.

If you choose the latter, your life will never be the same again.

It will be unfair, BUT if you pass the test, and die to your flesh, you would have uprooted such a curse in your life. You will discover that what you receive in return far outweighs the price of your pride.

You will discover anointings, favor, blessing and miracles on the other side. You will be amazed to discover how much of a blockage satan has been using this repeated sin in your life, to stop the blessings of God from reaching you. You will be amazed at how much demonic activity this sin of yours, has given license to.

By making the right choice, you uproot this pattern and make room for abundant blessings that have been there all along.

EXTRA NOTES

Chapter 12

Step-by-Step Solutions

Chapter 12 – Step-by-Step Solutions

Chapter Reference: *Strategies of War*, Chapter 5

So, how do you break through to victory? How do you deal with generational curses? A good place to start would be to identify them in the first place. Trust me, when you ask the Lord to show you, He will show you.

For many people, they see the curses. In fact, even the world sees it. They just call it hereditary sickness and disease. We know what that is. It is a curse that has been passed down from generation to generation.

DEALING WITH GENERATIONAL CURSES

STEP 1: TAKE OWNERSHIP

What habits are you doing that were the same as your forefathers? Ladies and gentlemen, if you see a generational curse in your life, it is time to take ownership of it. There is something very powerful about that and I am speaking from my own experience.

When I said, "This is my father's curse, my grandfather's curse, or my father's sin," I always felt so powerless to do something about it. I felt like the boxer in 1 Corinthians 9 hitting the air.

I never felt like I was connecting with satan's jaw. I was just punching around trying to do warfare against everything in order to get a victory. Then, one day the Lord said, "You take ownership and responsibility for this sin."

Remember that old song, "It's not my mother nor my sister, but it's me oh Lord, standing in the need of prayer"? The Lord brought me to my knees and said, "You take ownership. This is not their curse or any of your ancestor's curse. It is your curse."

I permitted this in my life. All I needed to do was apply James 4:7 to my life. *"Therefore submit to God. Resist the devil and he will flee from you."* Once you have taken ownership, you are holding that sin in your hand and guess what?

You can put it under the blood and wash it away. While it is your dad's sin, your mom's sin, or your grandfather's sin, you cannot do anything with it. I cannot wash away their sin. That is for Christ to do, not me.

However, I can bring my sin to Christ. I can put my responsibility under the blood and be redeemed. I can ask for forgiveness and I can submit to the Lord. So, that is what you need to do.

STEP 2: APPLY THE BLOOD

You say, "Father, forgive me for I have sinned. Yes, we may have a curse of poverty in my family, but Lord there was a time when I blamed you for that poverty and that was sin.

There was a time when you told me to walk in faith, but I did not, I walked in fear and that which is not of faith is sin. Father, forgive me for not walking in faith. Forgive me for doubting you. Forgive me for blaming you and getting bitter towards you.

By getting bitter and angry, I made that sin my own and I brought that curse upon myself. I repent Father. Satan, I close that door and I chop down this tree and you will get out of my life right now.

I remove the spirit of poverty and I tell it to be gone in Jesus' name. I am not accepting it anymore."

STEP 3: RENEW YOUR MIND

When people are dealing with generational sins and curses, I tell them that for the first while they will probably have to pray about it daily. Why? It is because that curse shaped the way you think.

It is not good enough even after praying and repenting. You have to stop thinking that way. You have to stop giving that soil fertilizer for the seed to keep growing. The way that you think and act keep leading you down this sinful road.

You have to be transformed by the renewing of your mind. If you want to break free of generational curses, be transformed by the renewing of your mind. Think a different way and you will not keep falling into the same sin again and again.

Sure, you could just stand against that sin in your will power. You can do it, but it is going to be hard. It is easier to say, "Lord, change me. Let me be clay on the potter's wheel. Change the way I think, so that I do not think this way anymore.

Give me a new way. Replace my doubt with faith, and my fear with love. Replace this way of thinking that it is you doing these bad things to me. Replace these things with the truth, so that I can be set free Lord."

Spiritual Discernment Workshop

When you do that, not only will you break free of the generational sin, but you will not pass it onto the generations after you. You will become a different person. For those of you in apostolic training - a lot of this should be making sense.

Suddenly, you understand why the Lord said that He wants you to let go of family and let go of your country. Why does the Lord do that to apostles? It is because you need to break free of those generational sins.

You cannot keep passing them onto your children, spiritual or natural. You have to break free, which means that you have to become a different person so that you do not fall into the same trap again and again.

So, put your sin under the blood and tell the enemy to flee. Then, let the work begin and start changing your habits so that you do not keep doing the same thing that you have been doing.

CHANGE - THE KEY TO VICTORY

What has been happening up until now? You sin and then you repent and tell the devil to go and then you sin again. If you keep going on like that, you will get victory, but that is like running a race with your feet tied together.

You are going to exhaust yourself. Why don't you just change? Then, you will not sin in the same way anymore and you will not have this curse anymore. It is easy. Just stop doing that thing you keep doing that keeps opening the door to the enemy.

Every time you do that thing, you give flight to the curse. You think, "Perhaps, no one saw me sin?" Well, someone did see it. The devil is only too glad when you fall into your usual sin trap. So, stop it and change who you are.

If you keep falling into the same sin again and again in a certain environment, get into another environment. Have a mentor get on you to change and put pressure on you. Get a spiritual parent that can give you another way to think and act, so that you can deal with the sin in you and deal with those sinful mindsets.

That is how you deal with generational curses.

DEALING WITH LEAVEN

STEP 1: BREAK SPIRITUAL LINKS

Now, when it comes to dealing with leaven, you have to disassociate yourself spiritually from your brother that is not walking in the light. That does not mean that you need to reject him.

It means that you love him, but you are not going to take his nonsense. It is like Jude 1:22-23 says,

> *And on some have compassion, making a distinction;*
> *23 but others save with fear, pulling them out of the fire, hating even the garment defiled by the flesh*

Love them, but hate the stain of sin because the stain of sin is like a contaminate or mold. It is leaven that spreads and destroys. It brings all twenty of those curses that I spoke about.

SIN MUSTN'T BE "LOVED"

People have this strange idea in both the world and in the church. "If you really love me, you would understand. You would just accept that this is the way that I am."

The truth is - I love you. I hate the stain of sin.

The Bible does not say that I have to love your sin. I am sorry, but the Bible says that I have to love you and I do. I love this little quirkiness about you. I love your heart for the Lord. I love how you always make me laugh, and that you are always there for me.

I love you, but I hate your rebellion, your jealousy, your fornication, and your adultery. I do not have to love your sin. The Bible does not tell me to love your sin.

The minute you accept and receive someone's sin, you receive the curse along with it. That is why it is so important when you have received a contamination from someone to search your own heart. Why are you so quick to agree with their sin and be a partaker of it?

Is there something that you need? Are you looking to them to meet a need in your heart that only the Lord can meet? Are you looking to this person to accept you in only a way that the Lord can accept you?

STEP 2: IDENTIFY YOUR NEED

Do you have a take/take relationship with this person? If so, that is your open door right there. No one should be meeting that need except the Lord. This is probably one of the biggest ways to pick up a curse from someone else. It is by needing them for something only the Lord can give you.

As believers, we should always be pouring and giving out. This is actually one of the easiest curses to deal with. Do you know what usually happens? You meet an old friend, you chat and share. The time was so good, but then on your way home, your car breaks down.

Once you get home, your stove blows up and then your child calls you and they are sick at school. You think, "What just happened? Out of the blue, so many things just started going wrong."

You just took on a bit of leaven. That is what happened. It is very easy to deal with this. You just need to break links. "Father, I disassociate myself with that sin. In Jesus' name, I speak blessing on that person, but I do not accept that sin.

I pray, Holy Spirit, that you take them where they need to go and that you deal with them accordingly so that they can come in line, but I am not partaking and fellowshipping with that sin. I am not bringing it into my home and making it a part of my life."

It does not mean that you reject them, but you certainly do not accept or feel sorry for their actions, because every one of us in this world has the freedom to choose. They can choose to sin or not to sin.

Each of us walks out our own walk before God in fear and trembling. It is not for you to walk their road. It is for them to walk their road. Leave them to walk it and you walk yours.

DEALING WITH PERSONAL SIN

Then, there is dealing with personal sin. Again, this one is very easy. You see your sin and you see the pattern through your life. You always responded to the same thing in the same way.

STEP 1: GO BACK TO THE BEGINNING AND REPENT

Go back to the very first thing that happened and repent. "Lord, when those kids were bullying me, I know that I made a judgment in my heart. I know that I wanted to turn around and punch them in the nose.

I was so angry, so violently angry. Forgive me Lord, because every time I am under pressure, I respond the same way. I always respond in bitterness. Forgive me Lord."

If there is someone that you can pray with, have them go into those memories with you and speak the healing as well. Say, "Satan, that door that I gave you access through, I close it. You loose your hold and get out of here."

STEP 2: CHANGE YOUR HABITS

Then, change your habits. When you find yourself in that same situation and you feel that temptation to respond in the same way, do not do it. If you really want to break free, in the heat of the moment, make a new decision and create a new righteous template, instead of a sinful one, and you will break free.

The great thing is that the blessing of the Lord is like a river in flood, and the curses that the enemy uses are like a beaver dam that blocks up that blessing. If you just take down the dam, that river will flow.

Here you are thinking that you have to travail and beg God for His blessing, but He is telling you to simply stand under the waterfall. His blessing is there. You have access to His storehouse.

Deal with the curses and the blessing will come naturally. You do not have to keep begging God to bless you. He has blessed you with every blessing. When Jesus went to the cross, He gave you everything that the Father has.

You do not have to keep asking God for blessing. You have to figure out what is stopping that blessing. You have to put it under His blood and then the blessing will flow again. If you are experiencing curses in your life, then deal with them and walk in blessing.

PRACTICAL PROJECT

1. Make a list of the curses in your life from the twenty that I named in Chapter 2. Which category do they fall into?

    a. Personal Sin

        i. You are the only one in your family who has it
        ii. You are the only one out of everyone you know who has it
        iii. The only other people you see it in are your children

    b. Generational Curses

        i. Pattern in your family
        ii. Had it before you can remember
        iii. Was always with you
        iv. Grew into it

    c. Leaven of Others

        i. Curse manifested after being with someone
        ii. Old friends, ministers, mentors... someone you submitted to

2. Identify when each one of these curses began.

3. Repentance

I do not know about you, but there is nothing like a good conviction. It helps you to break free and let go of those loads. There is no greater feeling than to be able to come to the cross and lay those loads down especially when the enemy has been accusing you, you have been having doubts, and people have been speaking against you. You just feel so loaded down.

When that happens, there is a temptation to try and justify yourself. You should rather run to the cross and repent. It only takes five minutes. His blood is always there and it is always available to you.

If it is a personal sin, ask the Lord to forgive you. Go back to where you first started this pattern in your life, where you repeated the same sin and ask Him for forgiveness.

Identify that open door and actually you should take time daily to repent. Matthew 6:9-13 says,

> *In this manner, therefore, pray: Our Father in heaven, hallowed be Your name.*
> *10 Your kingdom come. Your will be done on earth as it is in heaven.*
> *11 Give us this day our daily bread.*
> *12 And forgive us our debts, as we forgive our debtors.*
> *13 And do not lead us into temptation, but deliver us from the evil one. For Yours is the kingdom and the power and the glory forever. Amen.*

It goes onto say that if you do not forgive your brother, God will not forgive you. In other words, ask for forgiveness for your sins and forgive others as well. This is a daily prayer.

Seeking the Lord for His blessing every day is so simple. Lay those sins down. It does not have to be a whole big travail. Just put them under the blood. Don't do it because God needs you to. He got the memo two thousand years ago.

It's you who needs to put those sins under the blood, so that your heart is no longer condemned and you can go to the Throne with boldness.

Also, you need to do it so that satan does not have a foothold in your life. Is that not worth it? Then, when you are repenting of generational sins, take ownership of them, identify when you made the curse your own, and repent.

The same goes for the leaven of others. Find out where you opened the door, where you allowed that sin into your life, and get yourself a new lump. Ask the Lord to purge you, to help you to let go and see through His eyes, and to minister and bless His people effectively.

QUICK NOTE ON DOCTRINE

I also want to mention that the leaven of others also includes teachings that you receive in your spirit from people that were not exactly in right standing with God. This comes from doctrines that were heretical or teachings from someone who has a contamination in their spirit.

When you receive those things in your life, you walk in the curse as well. You can simply say, "Lord, forgive me for getting into that teaching. I should not have done that. I knew better than to watch that movie or to receive that thing into my heart."

It does not have to be a drama. This is a daily, simple thing. That is the balance that I hope to bring about curses. I know that this is very intense and can be broken down in so many different parts, but more than anything, I want to leave you with hope.

You do not have to suffer anymore. You do not have to be poor anymore. You do not have to be sick anymore, and you do not have to pass these things down to your children.

You have the power in His blood to stop it dead in its tracks. So, do that. Lay the axe to those roots. Wash out the stain of sin that is in your life and you will walk in the abundance of blessing that God has given to you as an inheritance.

This chapter was taken from the book *Strategies of War* written by Colette Toach.

SCRIPTURES TO MEMORIZE

Proverbs 25:28 *In this manner, therefore, pray: Our Father in heaven, hallowed be Your name.*

10 Your kingdom come. Your will be done on earth as it is in heaven.

11 Give us this day our daily bread.

12 And forgive us our debts, as we forgive our debtors.

13 And do not lead us into temptation, but deliver us from the evil one. For Yours is the kingdom and the power and the glory forever. Amen.

KEY PRINCIPLES

Generational Curses:

- ✓ Take ownership
- ✓ Apply the Blood
- ✓ Renew your mind

Leaven of Others:

- ✓ Break spiritual links
- ✓ Identify your need

Personal Sin:

- ✓ Go back to the beginning and repent
- ✓ Change your habits

EXTRA NOTES

BONUS CHAPTER

DEALING WITH A BACKLASH

Bonus Chapter – Dealing With a Backlash

Chapter Reference: An article written by Craig Toach

We cannot begin to tell you how many times prophets have written us and said: "I ministered to someone who was sick or in bondage and I was barely out the door when everything began going wrong in my life!" Some came down with the same physical symptoms, some experienced strife in their homes, some theft, some destruction... cars breaking down, accidents, sickness, appliances breaking, children getting hurt... the list is endless!

This article by Apostle Craig Toach specifically covers dealing with a backlash after ministering to an individual. This includes personal ministry, prayer by the laying on of hands and intercession on behalf of another.

WHAT JUST HAPPENED?

I am sure that everyone at one time or another has taken a good hard look at the world in which we live in. You have seen the lonely; you have seen the lost and the hurting and have felt the heart of Jesus crying out to see them healed. You have said: "Send me Lord I will go!"

As your earnest cry went out, so the Lord has brought you those to whom you have ministered to. Their lives have been changed and you have seen them grow from strength to strength and you feel on top of the world.

Yet there are times when you have ministered forth and then found yourself under the greatest of attacks! It is like you have stirred up a beehive and everything seems to be coming at you. Everything seems to go wrong and you are left wondering, "what exactly happened there?" Well you have just experienced a backlash in the spirit! Today I would like to show you what a backlash is, how it happens and what you can do to stop it from happening to you.

WHAT IS A BACKLASH?

It is a common belief that if you have prayed or ministered for someone and you come under a spiritual attack it means that you have really made the devil mad and you are on your way to victory.

You know the old idea that if you want to get honey from a beehive and you make them mad they will come and get you! That is a lie from the pit of hell and it is a weapon that the enemy is using to stop the church form being victorious.

Colette Toach

So what is a backlash? Well very simply put, it is a spiritual attack a person will come under after they join their hearts and spirits with another person who is under a curse.

HOW DOES IT HAPPEN?

Backlashes happen in two ways:

THROUGH CONTAMINATION

The first, is through spiritual contamination. Have you ever seen a blood transfusion take place? In the early days of medicine, what happened was that if someone needed blood, two people with the same blood types would be put next to each other and a tube placed into each of their veins. And so blood would be transferred from one to the other.

The problem with this was that if there were any viruses in one person's blood they could travel in the tube between them and go into the other person and thus infect them too.

Well this is what is it like when you minister to someone. In the spirit you open you heart to the person you are ministering to and link with them in the spirit. Now as you flow out to them you are doing a kind of spiritual blood transfusion.

As you minister - what is happening is that you are pouring forth the healing, revelation and anointing into that person, but because you are also opening up yourself to them and they are pouring into you in turn.

Now if you are not careful the very contamination they have in their spirit will be transferred into yours and it won't take long before you start show the symptoms. If you minister to someone with an addiction, you might find yourself craving for that very same thing. It they were under a curse in any way, you might start to see yourself come under that same curse. Now you can see why it is written:

> *1 Timothy 5:22 Do not lay hands on anyone hastily, nor share in other people's sins; keep yourself pure*

THROUGH REJECTION

The second way of receiving a backlash is by rejection of your ministry. I am sad to say that your ministry will not always be accepted. There are many reasons, but the two most common ways are either, that the person did not ask for ministry, but you ministered anyway or that they did not believe what you had to say.

What happens is that the very demon you where supposed to deal with and set that person free from, will later on attack you. You see unless the person you are ministering to closes the door to the evil influence you have no right to interfere.

Would you have the cheek to go to your neighbor's house and tell his party guests to go home? No, you have no right and until the neighbor gives you that right, you are looking for trouble. Well the spiritual side in no different. That is why it says:

> ***Matthew 10:14*** *And whoever will not receive you nor hear your words, when you depart from that house or city, shake off the dust from your feet*

So if you are to minister forth and help the lost and hurting, how can you do this without receiving that backlash?

HOW DO YOU PREVENT IT?

There is a very quick and simple solution that you need to follow but before I go into it I would like to show you why you need to apply this solution every time you minister forth.

In the case of the spiritual transfusion, you have now poured forth what the Lord has given you. You have followed through to the end and you can see the victory. At this point many people just leave it at that and do not take the tube that is linking them together away. So what happens is you are still linked to each other and are still flowing into each other.

You need to take that tube away and purify yourself from any contamination. Otherwise all you will do is spread it around to anyone else you minister to.

In the case of the person rejecting your ministry, they have opened the door to a curse and to the enemy. With you ministering to them you have in a sense partaken of that curse and come under it's influence. You need to get rid of that curse so that you can be free to carry on without being hindered in any way.

Well unlike the natural, the spiritual realm plays by a different set of rules. You do not have to be contaminated or come under anyone's curse! And this can be all done by prayer. Prayer you might ask? Yes, it is as simple as that, no need to fast or to go into quarantine!

As you leave the home of the person all you need do is break spiritual links and renounce anything you might have picked up. A simple prayer of:

> *"Father I submit myself to you and break all spiritual links with this person.*
>
> *I renounce any contamination or curse I might have received from them.*

Colette Toach

In Jesus Name

Amen"

By doing this you are clearing your spirit and stopping the enemy from gaining a hold in your life. If you do this every time you finish ministering, you will never experience a backlash in the spirit again. And should you forget to do it right away and things get a little out of hand. Well it is never to late to say that simple prayer.

You are called to be a spiritual doctor, to take care of the sick and hurting. You are called to free them from the bondages that hold them back. You have the answers they need and can fix any problem! But you need to ask yourself this question:

If even in the natural worldly doctors always look after their own health and safety first to be more affective - should you not to do the same for your patients?

SCRIPTURES TO MEMORIZE

1 Timothy 5:22 *Do not lay hands on anyone hastily, nor share in other people's sins; keep yourself pure.*

Matthew 10:14 *And whoever will not receive you nor hear your words, when you depart from that house or city, shake off the dust from your feet*

KEY PRINCIPLES

- ✓ A backlash is a spiritual attack a person will come under after they join their hearts and spirits with another person who is under a curse.
- ✓ A backlash occurs through contamination and rejection of your ministry.
- ✓ Prevent a backlash by breaking spiritual links.

About the Author

Born in Bulawayo, Zimbabwe and raised in South Africa, Colette had a zeal to serve the Lord from a young age. Coming from a long line of Christian leaders and having grown up as a pastor's kid, she is no stranger to the realities of ministry. Despite having to endure many hardships such as her parent's divorce, rejection, and poverty, she continues to follow after the Lord passionately. Overcoming these obstacles early in her life has built a foundation of compassion and desire to help others gain victory in their lives.

Since then, the Lord has led Colette, with her husband Craig Toach, to establish *Apostolic Movement International,* a ministry to train and minister to Christian leaders all over the world, where they share all the wisdom that the Lord has given them through each and every time they chose to walk through the refining fire in their personal lives, as well as in ministry.

In addition, Colette is a fantastic cook, an amazing mom to not only her 4 natural children, but to her numerous spiritual children all over the world. Colette is also a renowned author, mentor, trainer and a woman that has great taste in shoes! The scripture to "be all things to all men" definitely applies here, and the Lord keeps adding to that list of things each and every day.

How does she do it all? Experience through every book and teaching the life of an apostle firsthand, and get the insight into how the call of God can make every aspect of your life an incredible adventure.

Read more at www.colette-toach.com

Connect with Colette Toach on Facebook! www.facebook.com/ColetteToach

Check Colette out on Amazon.com at: www.amazon.com/author/colettetoach

EXCERPTS TAKEN FROM THE FOLLOWING BOOKS

If you enjoyed these excerpts, feel free to purchase the books at our bookshop or at Amazon.com.

PROPHETIC WARRIOR

Book 5 of the Prophetic Field Guide Series

By Colette Toach

A true warrior holds no excuses of why he cannot defeat his enemy and so is true with a genuine prophet of God. He is ready to take up the weapons of warfare that God has prepared for Him and to set the captive free and to heal the broken hearted.

The prophet that God has called is ready to step onto the battlefield, gain victory in their own lives, and then share the secrets to obtaining victory to all those around them.

Prophet of God, now is the time to face your own limitations and your own bondages and to see what has been holding you back from walking as the warrior that God has called you to be.

Bookshop US: www.ami-bookshop.com/index.php?Product=4

Bookshop SA: www.amisa-bookshop.com/index.php?Product=4

Amazon.com: www.amazon.com/author/colettetoach

PROPHETIC COUNTER INSURGENCE

Book 6 of the Prophetic Field Guide Series

By Colette Toach

Learn all about the "prophetic super spy", discover strategies that can be used in spiritual warfare, receive stealth training, find the secrets to dealing with fear of the mind, and where spiritual warfare begins and ends.

It is time to become an agent of Christ, capable of striking down the enemy at any time, in any place, and wherever the Lord calls for it. It is time to take the crippling blows of the enemy and turn them into deathly blows of destruction.

Bookshop US: www.ami-bookshop.com/index.php?Product=1009

Bookshop SA: www.amisa-bookshop.com/index.php?Product=993

Amazon.com: www.amazon.com/author/colettetoach

Excerpts Taken From the Following Books

THE MINISTER'S HANDBOOK

By Colette Toach

This is your manual on effective ministry. Whether you are dealing with an unexpected demon manifestation or you need to give marital counsel, you will find the answers here.

Colette Toach gives it to you in plain language. She gives you the steps 1, 2, 3 of how to do what God has called you to do. Keep a copy on hand, because you will come back to it time and time again!

Bookshop US: www.ami-bookshop.com/index.php?Product=887

Bookshop SA: www.amisa-bookshop.com/index.php?Product=887

Amamzon.com: www.amazon.com/author/colettetoach

PROPHETIC ESSENTIALS

Book 1 of the Prophetic Field Guide Series

By Colette Toach

In this book, you will find out that the call of the prophet goes far deeper than the functions and duties that the prophet fulfills. Anyone flowing in prophetic ministry can carry out tasks similar to the prophet.

If it burns in you to pay any price that is necessary and to stand up and break down the barriers between the Lord Jesus and His Bride, then my friend, you have picked up the right tool that will confirm the fire in your belly and the call of God on your life.

Bookshop US: www.ami-bookshop.com/index.php?Product=58

Bookshop SA: www.amisa-bookshop.com/index.php?Product=58

Amazon.com: www.amazon.com/author/colettetoach

THE WAY OF DREAMS AND VISIONS

By Colette Toach

This book is the key that will open up the door to the realm of the spirit for you. Whether you have just come to know the Lord or have been saved for many years, you will find a treasure map in each page of this book, opening up the things that God is telling you RIGHT NOW!

Understand the secrets in your dreams and come to a place of confidence in the future God has set for you and a peace in knowing that He is in control of your life!

Bookshop US: www.ami-bookshop.com/index.php?Product=6
Bookshop SA: www.amisa-bookshop.com/index.php?Product=6
Amazon.com: www.amazon.com/author/colettetoach

STRATEGIES OF WAR

By Colette Toach

Warfare is a very important part of our Christian lives. Whether we know it or not, the enemy is always looking for a way to take down the children of God. Now it is time that you learned how to stop taking the hits and take the fight to him instead.

No more allowing the enemy to have his way. Take back your land and remove him from your life for good.

Your victory is at hand. So, take hold and allow Colette Toach to guide and teach you the strategy to tearing down the kingdom of darkness

Bookshop US: www.ami-bookshop.com/index.php?Product=1014
Bookshop SA: www.amisa-bookshop.com/index.php?Product=1000
Amazon.com: www.amazon.com/author/colettetoach

Excerpts Taken From the Following Books

THE WAY OF DREAMS AND VISIONS STUDENT MANUAL

By Colette Toach

There are secrets in your dreams. The Lord is trying to speak to you, and as a prophet, these messages are clearer and more frequent. Going way beyond just simple dream interpretation, Colette Toach teaches you how to minister using dream interpretation by the spirit.

You will go beyond just understanding your own dreams, as Colette divulges everything she has learned in how to interpret for others. Imagine that you are sitting relaxed in your lounge, while she shares with you everything you are likely to face, and how to deal with it when it comes to dream interpretation.

With this kit, you will gain a new understanding of not only your dreams, but of the Lord himself.

Bookshop US: http://ami-bookshop.com/index.php?Product=760

Bookshop SA: www.amisa-bookshop.com/index.php?Product=760

PRACTICAL PROPHETIC MINISTRY STUDENT MANUAL

By Colette Toach

If you have a desire to serve the Lord and feel a fire burning in your heart for the prophetic, then you want to get your hands on this manual.

But let me warn you, if you really delve into this, it will not remain some great theory you just learn about - this will transform your life! The ride might get a bit bumpy and this stuff is hazardous to your flesh. But you are a prophet, so you are definitely asking for that kind of trouble (smile).

In this manual you will find your prophetic mentor in a very compacted and handy format. Colette Toach has poured all her wisdom, all of her anointing and all of her little gems that she has collected over the years in here. So you will get something others do not get. On each page you will feel an impartation of the Lord's power as you open your heart to receive.

Bookshop US: www.ami-bookshop.com/index.php?Product=763

Bookshop SA: www.amisa-bookshop.com/index.php?Product=763

CONTACT INFORMATION UNITED STATES

To check out our wide selection of materials, go to: www.ami-bookshop.com

Do you have any questions about any products?

Contact us at: +1 (760) 466 -7679
(9am to 5pm California Time, Weekdays Only)

E-mail Address: admin@ami-bookshop.com

Postal Address:

> A.M.I.
> 5663 Balboa Ave #416
> San Diego, CA 92111, USA

Facebook Page: http://www.facebook.com/ApostolicMovementInternational

YouTube Page: https://www.youtube.com/c/ApostolicMovementInternational

Twitter Page: https://twitter.com/apmoveint

Amazon.com Page: www.amazon.com/author/colettetoach

AMI Bookshop – It's not Just Knowledge, It's **Living Knowledge**

CONTACT INFORMATION SOUTH AFRICA

To check out our wide selection of materials, go to: www.amisa-bookshop.com

Do you have any questions about any products?

Contact us at: 071 056 6321
(Tuesday – Friday, 8am to 5pm South Africa Standard Time)

E-mail Address: admin@amisa-bookshop.com

Facebook Page: https://www.facebook.com/ApostolicMovementSouthAfrica

YouTube Page: https://www.youtube.com/c/ApostolicMovementInternational

Twitter Page: https://twitter.com/amiafrica

Amazon.com Page: www.amazon.com/author/colettetoach

AMI Bookshop – It's not Just Knowledge, It's **Living Knowledge**